i

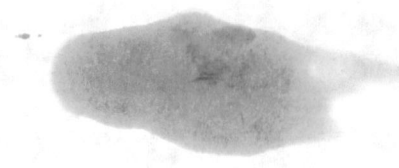

Socialism & Democracy

Sarah P. Condor-Fisher

Socialism & Democracy

Copyright ©2016 by Sarah P. Condor-Fisher, Ph.D., Esq., LL.M.

6.0" x 9.0" (15.25 x 22.86 cm)

Black on White Paper

250 pages

ISBN-13: 978-1530995745

ISBN-10: 1530995744

Printed in the United States of America

v

Contents:

The Wall   1

Why Vote?   4

What Is Socialism about?   6

Is Capitalism Compatible with Socialism?   13

An Act of Love?   19

Democracy v. Theocracy   21

The Rise of Factions:

       What is "Social" – Democracy?   24

Everyone is a Man of Faith   29

On Bolsheviks, Mensheviks and Factions   32

Socialism in America   37

What is a "Single Payer Healthcare" system?   42

Unfit for President   45

The Lure of Sugar Daddy Sanders   49

Who Is Sanders?   54

When Did We Start Looking up to Europe?   57

Clinton, Sanders, and the Threat of Communism   61

Who Is George Soros?   64

Democratic Socialism - 21st Century Socialism   67

The English Language and

       the Totality of Tolerance   71

Foreign Policy   76

Clash of Civilizations   82

Interventionism and Isolationism

In Our Foreign Policy 87

Welcome to the "Democratic" United States! 94

Political Correctness That Matters 100

How to Deal with Political Correctness 102

In God We Trust 105

Obama's Censorship:

      Political Correctness Come Full Circle 112

"Pro-Choice" and "Economic Refugee" –

      Words That Should Be Illegal 115

Oregon Farmers Represent US! 119

What Is Ideology? 123

On Principled Conservatism 131

Diversity Is Longing for "the Other" 136

Radicalization from Start to Finish 143

Democracy, Amnesty, Citizenship

      and Anchor Babies 147

Natural-Born 152

Is Donald Trump a Demagogue? 156

European Migrant Crisis:

      The Worm Is Squirming 158

Nothing Ever Happens 162

Regulated to Death 165

We Have a Strategy 168

Rationalizing Terror? 171

"Cut the Bullshit!" Says Israel's Culture Minister 176

Brussels - a City Divided 179

Romney's Ugly Horns 182

Obama in Cuba – Why?! 185

No Existential Threat? 189

NATO and Obama's "Cold Peace" 192

Obama's Winning Friends Is Making Enemies 196

Clinton's Corruption and Sanders' Communism 198

Gray Mouse of Socialism 202

Clinton's Corrupt Camp and the Panama Papers 206

Trump University 209

Trump's Foreign Policy Speech 214

Merry Christmas 218

Sen. Cruz Warns: Orwellian Censorship
of Obama's Administration Poses
Grave Risk to Our National Security 220

Who Is the New Mayor of London? 223

There Can Be No Capitalism, No Republic
– without Independence 226

Doping in Sport 228

Peyton Manning v. Al Jazeera 235

The Wall

I grew up in the country surrounded by a wall. It was called the "Iron Curtain," because it was not quite a wall. Yet, it kept us in. So today, when people say it is impossible, I draw a sigh and whisper to myself: "If they only knew…"

When I tried to escape, it was two in the morning and I thought it would be easy because I had been to that crossing before and knew it very well. There was a railroad ran through the border and a forest lay nearby. It was just a matter of getting there, getting through. What is more, I had my best friend Pete with me, which seemed to dissolve the worst of trepidation, at least for the moment.

Little did we know that "they" knew about us as soon as we entered the 5-mile border "perimeter" accessible only to locals and people who lived there and possessed a special "pass." Taking a bus and getting off within this perimeter was the first mistake. Everything and everyone was monitored. Mind you, there was no electronic surveillance then – just people, like the locals who knew one another all too well, and the bus driver, and the soldiers patrolling bus stops.

We were lucky in that the bus was nearly empty and there was no-one at the last bus-stop, from which we could see the official border crossing point. We were determined to avoid that and go straight through the field to the Austrian woods. "It's so easy!" we laughed as we got off the bus, literally within reach of Austria. Little did we know…

It was a flatly plowed field with elevated guard posts, similar to what foresters and game hunters have. We knew those posts were monitoring nearly a mile each way and could not see us at night. We also knew there would be several fences to scale, for which purpose Pete had his wire cutters. We had a bag of food and a bag of clothes. We were both Olympic athletes and could outrun and outjump probably every soldier in the commie army. The service was compulsory and most men "did" those one-and-a-half years

1

drinking beer and playing cards. No incentive, initiative, discipline.

What we did not know was that border guards were patrolling with loaded machine guns and German Shepherds in pairs of two soldiers who were all selected based on their parents' communist allegiance. They let us walk just as far as they wanted and could have shot us at will without warning at any time. We were lucky the two guys, perhaps two years older than ourselves, did not shoot us but shouted first.

Still, I will never forget staring into the muzzle of a machine gun, answering questions about what I was doing. Illegally crossing the border was a crime against the Regime and the Party. It was as bad as it gets, murder, felony of the highest order! My throat was dry, Pete was white as a sheet, stammering like Ed Carney caught red-handed in his boss' office. Before we knew it, we were separated, strip-searched and cross-interrogated in cross-beams of 200W lamps with rough commie military voices firing from the dark questions to which I had no answers – absurd questions too, which were not questions at all, such as: "Do not lie to us, we know all about you!" and "Admit you were intentionally spying on military installations!"

When my eyes adjusted a little, they moved the lamps still closer. Although I was half-naked and it was cold in there, I felt sweat running down my forehead and my sides, everywhere.. I glimpsed two soldiers by the door with machine guns at the ready. It was a plain room in the cellar of the border barracks – whitewashed walls, dark brown wooden table, two chairs. One interrogator was behind me, one in front of me, my back was pressed against the table. In 30 minutes, I was ready to sign my name to a tightly-typed confession without being able to read a word, even had they given me a minute to peruse it, which they did not. They threw me in a stone-cold cell and let me beg for water for two hours.

In the morning, we were transported in a World War II Jeep with wooden planks for seats and two armed soldiers by each side to the KGB Headquarters in Bratislava. Further interrogation followed, then we were officially reprimand by the KGB Chief, who prided himself on being a former boxing champion. The little Napoleon of KGB was not pleased, he said, to see two members of the National and Olympic Team "disappoint the State, which had invested you with so much resources, money and trust! You know what you have done?! You betrayed the trust of the working people of this country, who have to struggle and slog away for you, the elite of the Nation to live in the lap of luxury…!"

Obviously, the man had no idea how we had lived: in a prison complex within the Prison State, fed on bread with lard and hamburgers from the worst ground beef you can imagine, swimming in fat. Yes, our dorm rooms in the complex called "Olympic Sports Institute" (referred to by all the Team Members as "the Lager" – German for concentration camp) were not much different from that interrogation room in the barracks basement. Frankly, the interrogators' voices resembled our Comrade Head Coach's voice during the 3-hour workouts when we fought to survive through cramps and pain twice a day… "You'll be here till you're sweating blood!!!" he yelled, my ears popped, and I whispered: "Yes Comrade Coach."

You see, it was not quite a wall which kept us in, yet being "walled in" is probably the best term I can think of. Then again, there are walls and there are walls. It starts brick by brick: political correctness is one, political allegiance to an -ism is another… until one day you realize that it is the wall they made you build around your own mind. The wall of guilt, hatred, self-doubt and fear which keeps you in.

Why Vote?

Once you start renaming mountains that had been dedicated to assassinated presidents and exhuming great generals from the greatest war that made your country, is that the beginning of an end? There is something rotten in the state of D.C.

I asked a Hispanic person, US citizen, why he did not vote. He said: "What's the point? There will always be someone who thinks about their own pocket and doesn't care. What has changed for me?"

When I was growing up in 1984, the land of double-speak and Big Brother, my parents had to vote for either one communist or another communist. There was one communist censored newspaper, two communist censored T.V. channels. I was too young to vote, of course, but they made me a member of the Communist Youth whether I wanted it or not. Once, I spent the money for membership stamps on food and got a B in morals.

Why vote? Democracy is founded on the ballot, once people stop to vote, democracy ceases to exist. If you are not interested in who administers the country and makes laws, why should they be interested in you? One of the virtues of democracy is the avoidance of dictatorship, which also means preventing revolutions and violent overthrows of the government.

Once, in a radio interview, I said that presidential candidates should avoid using the profane term "silent majority." Why? It is a negative term, imputing people powerlessness and inability to change things. This is a self-perpetuating, vicious circle. If you think you are powerless, then you are.

Democracy requires upward control and lower political sovereignty. Only people can effect change; and, indeed, only citizens should vote, because it is their state, nobody else's. Cleisthenes' democracy had it so, even in Rome, though the law of the blood became a second option

— not to vote, but to acquire citizenship: if one of your parents was a Roman citizen, you could become one too.

Citizenship is as important to democracy as air is to fire. It should not be granted lightly, for it is not taken away lightly. The larger the state (be it Roman Empire or the United States) the more citizens it contains, the more lengthy and complicated the election process. We should not be surprised at how vivid, vibrant and vociferous the process is. We should walk proudly to the ballot and tell the world: "This is how it's done!" Everything else is tyranny.

Perhaps not even all citizens should vote. There should be a voting test, in which you would prove your knowledge of history, political structure of the country, and mastership of English. You must be able to speak and understand the language in order to vote. Your knowledge of American history proves your love for the country.

Alas, much too low an emphasis has been placed on voting requirements: ID? Citizenship? Why, you do not even need to speak English to vote! How is that possible? Voting is a privilege and only those who earn it should be entitled to it.

What Is Socialism about?

Most of those who grew up in the capitalist West and do not entirely dislike the idea would answer: social equality, of course, what else? Some of the more radical ones would say "spreading wealth" or equality…

However, those are just words, phrases void of meaning, because there is no such thing as "equality" – we are all different. Equality of something? Perhaps. Equality of opportunity, equality of chance, equality in the right to compete: Get in the ring and fight!

Although it dates back as far as Plato, modern socialism took root with the French revolution: Equality, Liberty, Fraternity! Ah, those French, they have always had a penchant for pretty sounds and idealism. They gave us the Statue and with it came, well, a Trojan present, it seems, for the world is swarming with poor, huddled masses today. They have all heard of our Freedom, but what is it? Certainly not giving everybody what they want and letting them do as they please! For that is –

Yes, as someone who grew up in socialism, I can tell you what it is, what it results in – socialism, the very opposite of democracy. Let me tell you why.

Socialism consists: 1) censorship, total control of speech, political correctness regulated by the government, 2) central planning, by design from above, based not on the needs of the people but on what the demagogue in power says that (his) people need, 3) limited freedom of movement, 4) limited ability to achieve and prosper (speak of Pursuit of Happiness, ha!), 5) regulated market, thus limited economy and ability of the state (GDP, prosperity) to grow.

If you are able, capable, want to compete and conquer; if you are creative and want to exercise your freedom; if you are an intelligent, intellectual person who wants to think for himself or herself – socialism is not for you.

If you are someone who just wants to be and let be, has minimum interests in life and wants only a shelter and something to eat, a mandatory vacation once, twice a year, guaranteed minimum wages, no matter what you do or how hard you work (or do not work), long hospital lines with the same fed-up "doc" at the end of the day, grocery lines packed with hangdog faces, shabby houses no-one cares for (because everything belongs to everyone), oh well, then socialism is for you.

Beware! You can get there by electing your demagogue. You can get back only by a violent revolution, by overthrowing him and abolishing and demolishing the tyranny, for that is what socialism is. Naturally, you will be walking the tightrope of anarchy at all times during your struggle to re-acquire, re-conquer the freedoms you so blithely gave away.

Adjectives like "intellectual" or "catholic" are terms of insult and opprobrium in socialism, for it is the proletariat, the "working class" that stands above all doctors and lawyers and architects. "True Architect is the people," says the Demagogue. "The individual does not matter! One-two-four got killed? What difference does it make? I rule the people! They elected me to rule! Make no mistake, I am in power!"

Elections? There is one party and one Rule in socialism. Elections exist, to be sure, but they consist of coming to the ballot box to openly show support to the One. If you do not, he will crush you! You may "disappear" overnight without anyone ever hearing from you again. You think that Secret Police cannot enter your house without your permission? You think that you have to have right to an attorney? You think they cannot arrest you for looking dirty at a cop? Think again! Socialism is a police state! You have no idea what it means? 1984, much too real for me to ever read again…

Let me tell you about the "state of equality." Socialism desires equality. Equality consists of a state of equal outcome, where everything is based on the NEED for an equal outcome. If you are a doctor and work twelve hours a day, your salary is the same as that of a shop assistant who works eight hours a day. As a shop assistant once told my mother (a physician who spent seven years of her life working shifts as a nurse while studying medicine at night): "We all have one mouth and two hands, why should you get paid more than I?" Teach that to two generations of people and it will take four generations to alter their (children's children's) thinking – if ever.

Plato had it right: democracy may easily turn into a totalitarian regime – because the power is vested in the people and the people may give it away – to a populist demagogue. It is the demagogue who will promise blue from the sky to them: education will be for free, healthcare will be for free, houses and accommodation will be provided by the government... What else do you want? Yes, that will be for free too and that one too.

What follows? The moment the demagogue acquires power, he will take away a few rights, just a few, such as by modifying the First Amendment, what you can say and what religion is allowed. You have to speak "equality" be "politically correct" and, above all, "make no mistake." The Second Amendment follows suit, for by taking away your means of self-defense, the demagogue becomes invincible. Of course, the demagogue will ask "you the people" for an armed car, guard and military detail at all times by his Palace. That is taken for granted and is promptly provided. Do democratic leaders not have the same?

The next step is to bit off the First a little more and have you worship the Party of the Demagogue, abandon all other Gods, all other idols. He is your God, He is your Idol. Have you ever heard of a personality cult? Stalin cult? I could mention someone else too... In 1986, I visited Rumania (one of the few allowed countries on the permitted Party "vacation list"). The streets were not lined with trees but with portraits of Ceausescu and communist mottos, even in the country. Good sounding mottos too: "Through Peace to Prosperity!" or "With Soviet Union to World Peace!" or "Communism Our Goal!" or "Through Socialism to Glittering Tomorrows!"

I grew up among these mottos too. What was even worse though was the people – totally indoctrinated! Naked children begging by the train. Why, I also came from socialism! Yes, but we were more to the west, we still had what to eat... The stores in Rumania in 1987 consisted of rows of toilet paper, rows of cans of beans, alcohol and an old man trying to sell dry, inedible stinking fish. The Black Sea was barren, dark, as if it reflected the country which shored it. Milk was provided in exchange for special tickets, which were distributed only to families with children once a month... Do I have to go on?

I was unlucky enough to suffer an ear infection while in Rumania. Had it happened at home, in Czechoslovakia, my mother (as a doctor) could have called an ear specialist and we could have brought her a bottle of wine and some chocolates. That way we would not have had to wait in line and she would surely have given me the one ointment prescribed by the state. Of course, there was a better one but it was manufactured in Switzerland and was not even available on the black market. You'd better not fall sick!

What happened in Rumania? There was a doctor who spoke German so we could get by. Her office looked like the holding cell where I later spent a few nights after my arrest for trying to "run away" from those kowtowing communist weasels. On the floor, there were a couple of rugs and a bucket, something you might use for washing a car. Next to it stood a small iron table with a tray and a couple of iron instruments, pliers, needles – I was surprised there was no hammer...

She looked at me, called on her bodybuilder nurse who grasped my head and said something in Rumanian which sounded like a Hitler speaking to his staff. Out of the corner of my eye, I saw this huge dirty syringe, I mean something you would use for a horse, holding probably half a liter of liquid. She stuck a large needle on it (which lay in the open in plain sight next to the plyers in the tray) with her bare hands and pushed the whole thing into my ear. The bodybuilder nurse was holding my head. Then they started squeezing the liquid into my ear. I felt it in my toes. The pain was unimaginable! I could not hear for three weeks thereafter... Well, my father gave her ten German Marks, all we had for emergency purposes (black market money), and I was "discharged."

The free healthcare you get in socialism is worth precisely what everything else you get "for free" is worth. You had better study medicine yourself or have a doctor in the family – else, in any case, just hope that you never need socialist healthcare. I did have an advantage, as I say, my mother being a physician, but we still had to bring bribes to the office and they could only do so much in terms of the communist market cures and medication...

In socialism, all competition in the market disappears: there is governmental monopoly on drugs, cars, food... If you want something better, you want the greengrocer to "save" and put aside three bananas for your children for Christmas, you have to find a way to "befriend" the grocer. I remember my father cutting thin slices of a banana on a small breadboard, arranging them on a plate with tiny squares of a Cuban orange. It was Christmas Eve and I was allowed to eat half the plate myself! My parents had each one quarter, about four slices of banana and a quarter of an orange. I know, it is hard to believe, but that is how I grew up: from flu to scarlet fever to bronchitis, to rickets – I was a sickly child, mainly because my parents were "intellectuals" with few contacts to the "working class" people who lived in the country and had their own chickens and even a cow and a pig... They ate rabbits and once we were invited (by one of my mother's patients) to a "pig killing" – which was a wonderful thing: I had a sausage for the first time in my life! And the boiled and fried pieces of fat tasted so gooood!

If I say that the socialist market consists of monopolies and lack of competition, that does not quite describe what my experience does, does it? I still have to say that: costs are established by the government, as is the product, the same for everyone – one or two brands of the car, television set, even the house furniture. You go visit your schoolmate at home – they will have exactly the same

10

furniture from the same company (which supports the Regime, the Party and has acquired the much-desired governmental monopoly) – consequently, everything looks familiar to you. You feel at home everywhere! Isn't that wonderful?

Yet, you do not have a home. Your home, your privacy, your dignity has been taken away from you. After a while, you cannot imagine anything else... Not until you take a peek into a West German catalog someone has smuggled into the country... Not until you (surreptitiously, at low volume at night) listen to the Russian-jammed Radio Free Europe...

Here is another aspect of socialism. Socialism is a police state. If a policeman stops you, you have to do as he says, go with him, stay locked up without any rights until he lets you go or you proceed to prison from which they pick you up and put you in front of a three-judge panel. Hopefully, these minions of the Regime will let you go...

Of course, if you have had the audacity to say something untoward about the government or the Demagogue – why, that is worse than a murder! Political prisoners are prisoners of free speech, the greatest evil of capitalism! The minimum sentence for "attacking the Regime" was 20 years, usually of hard labor, in a uranium mine (by then totally "mined out" by the Russians) or in a coal mine. Years later, after the "Velvet Revolution," I had a boyfriend who had these rather large black spots around his spine and lower and upper back. I asked him where they came from, what were they. He said he was doing forced labor in a coal mine for two years, a deep black coal mine in Northern Moravia. I asked no more.

Today, I look at the modern demagogue who grew up with all advantages of capitalism and what he – indeed, she too – knows about socialism is limited to sociology studies, books describing those wonderful ideals of Marx, Engels, Lenin and their followers). This Modern Demagogue says: I am a "democratic socialist" – just to confuse you. If it has "democratic" or "democrat," it must be good, mustn't it?

11

Allow me to explain: social democrats in western European political systems are innocent only because they play their "social role" and function as part of a multi-party parliamentarian political system. What is more, they are "social" democrats, not democratic socialists – a difference not without insignificance! The latter, a democratic socialist, obviously means that this Modern Demagogue is a socialist first and uses the "demos" – i.e. people – only as an adjectival premodifier to personal power, the power of a populist demagogue who will turn "demos" (people) into "agony" (struggle) at the very first opportunity, the moment they transfer their power to Him: the "Struggle of the Proletariat," Marx called it.

In a two party representative government, the danger of democracy turning into a totalitarian regime is much greater than in a multi-party parliamentarian system, where all powers and factions are kept in check by all the other powers and factions. As freedom is indispensable to democracy and it is also "to a faction as air is to fire" (as James Madison says in Federalist 10), we must treat democracy not as a stable system, a huge majestic animal without any natural enemies, but as a fragile, beautiful creature, a gentle lady, who can be swayed and lured, led astray and – violated – by a mob!

A mob is what people become in the hands of a socialist demagogue. There is no more "We the People." People do not matter. Mottoes and icons matter, banners and slogans which you must shout too – or else...

I shiver when I see it, I can smell it a thousand miles away. When you have seen the Heart of Darkness, it alters you forever. "We the Mob, We the Mob!" is ringing in my ears. Ah, but that was not the old communist T.V. – that was NBC! Really? Just think in silence, do not let it out; for if you refuse to be subdued, suppressed, refuse to conform and give away your rights and liberties for some larger abstract "good," off to the mine with you! Make no mistake about it: an individual "makes no difference!"

That is what socialism is about. Believe me, I have been there before – and I am not going back!

Is Capitalism Compatible with Socialism?

There are natural elements of "social ethics" in capitalism but these have nothing to do with socialism. If anything, although they have the same goal – to help the underprivileged and assist the disabled and poor – they approach this goal from a completely different end: the end which is the only long-term sustainable and enabling one. In other words, socialism gives you a fish at a time for a day or two, as the government deems proper – to everybody the same fish, no matter what they do or how hungry they are – whereas: capitalism teaches you how to fish.

Charities and foundations for the poor, great hospitals with superb state-of-the-art technology and care – those can only exist in capitalism because they are founded on care not mandated by the government but the care of the neighbor for the neighbor, out of love and happiness which is derived from such help. There is no happiness in socialist care, mandated by the government. Remember Confucius? He who is given is gifted once, he who has given is gifted twice. Think about it.

I recall Hayek writing that it is the most painful of feelings to watch how the socialist ideals aspiring to honest goals in helping humankind and direct them the right way wind up in the very opposite: destruction of liberty, personal freedom and happiness. Why? The person does not matter when what is good is directed from a governmental center. The apparatchik in the machinery of bureaucracy may have the best goals in mind, but no one single expert, no genius, not even the best of the best selected by some demagogue with a vision – can direct the economy and prosperity of a nation the way a market can do it on its own.

Free market and capitalist economy is the greatest superpower known to mankind. No super-computer we have developed can calculate, predict and plan – and regulate (!) – the way free market does. Will there be mistakes? Certainly, but the market has the ability to "equalize" itself. It will permit a company to grow only so long as the company provides the best services at the most economic level. The power of the company is not equal to its size. We are speaking about quality vs. quantity here. Once some centralized bureaucracy enters free market and begins to direct costs of goods, determining which company should survive and which should not, a vicious circle begins at the end of which there are no winners – though everyone may get a trophy for participation… That is what Hayek meant by his remark that it is very painful to watch the idealist socialists end with the very opposite they wanted: a dejected, unhappy crowd of grey people living in gray houses with their gray smiles leading miserable existence without purpose.

I may speak of companies, but companies are only people connected by a common purpose – to succeed, be the best on the market and produce value. Money is the by-product. The final product is personal happiness and satisfaction. Why does Charles Koch still work? It gives him pleasure and happiness. Government does not care for your personal happiness and satisfaction when it regulates the market. I wish I could show you the "candlestick scene" from Les Miserables: the old man (a bishop) catches a thief (the protagonist, Jean Valjean) stealing silverware from his house. Valjean slaps him and runs away. He is later apprehended and brought before the bishop to corroborate his identity as a thief. Instead, the bishop admonishes Valjean that he forgot to take also the candlesticks he had given him. This humbles Valjean and opens his eyes to a different world – the world where moral value and ethics need not be part of the state machinery and result in apprehension and sentencing: because there is no need to steal if kindness and openness of the others accepts and provides for one's own drawbacks, mishaps and insufficiencies. The bishop is a product of capitalist economy – he is rich and represents moral values of capitalism. Valjean is the victim of social neglect – the state that cannot take care of him and does not care for his happiness.

We should also never forget how our country was born – from the visceral struggle of two groups. First, the Leiden separatists, whom we refer to as Pilgrim Fathers. These were the people longing to be free and unencumbered by the heavy hand of some merciless monarch who had no interest in their success and personal happiness. They were excessively taxed and prevented from practicing not just their religious beliefs but their respective trades and occupations. Thus, they moved to the country with the most flourishing, free market economy at the time, Holland, before venturing (and it was a common joint venture based on a contract) to found a separate colony here.

The second group followed suit. Those were the Puritans and we all know who they were and why they came. Protestantism became an indelible, inseparable fabric of the character of this new man, this – American! Many of them followed Calvin and did not find James I a just king – and justice never mean fairness, but that is another matter.

Nothing was for free or freely given to them. They all had to struggle from day-to-day and fight for everything. As a result they had to "hang together" or else they would all "hang apart" – from the very start (yes, it was Ben Franklin, not Sam Adams or John Hancock who left us with the chopped up snake and the motto we should all stand by today). Looking back, some of us might view this "hanging together" as (to use a more modern term, popular in the 1980s Poland) "solidarity" and point out that the mutual support and cohesion wears nothing if not the cloak of "socialism."

Alas, I say, read again. Proverbs 11:24: "A man may give freely, and still his wealth will be increased; and another may keep back more than is right, but only comes to be in need." There goes another: "Those who give generously receive more, but those who are stingy with what is appropriate will grow needy." Ibid. No government will come and give you brass candlesticks, but if you need one, your neighbor will be happy to help – provided that you do not

15

take away his Bible and do not overtax his business to bankruptcy.

For you unbelievers – atheists – out there: the Bible is the key tome for Christians, Protestants, and many other denominations. I was brought up in a country which despised and scorned religion. I have never been taught how to pray. I was told religion was "an old wife's tale." When I first came to England (at the age of 17, after having also spent some time in a communist prison upon my arrest on the border, strip-search, cross-interrogation and that followed – see my book "Escape") I was asked what religion I was. I could not answer and the instinct instilled in me was to respond that I was an "atheist."

I said it proudly, the way I would have said it at school a year ago (a different response was impermissible and I would have been the butt-end of all the jokes of the class for years to come). To my astonishment, the circle of teenagers (and some parents) who surrounded me at this Plymouth soiree, gasped. Conversations ceased, even among the adults at the table. One could hear a needle drop. Did I say something bad? I blushed. "So you don't believe in God?" a girl asked me. I shook my head. "What do you believe in then?" she asked. I bit my tongue, not knowing what to say. "Evolution?" They did not want to embarrass me – they were just curious. To them, I was like a strange animal imported from far away, the land they would never know. (Thank God!)

Dear atheists, do not disparage what you do not know. That is the quintessence of ignorance: pretending that you know what you do not know instead of asking what and why. You can always start by taking the Bible as a pretty fairy tale. Are fairy tales not all we need to point our children in the right direction? Is all that we need to know about distinguishing between Good and Evil not anchored in our fairy tales?

No, I am not diverging. Look up Max Weber's "Protestant Ethic and the Spirit of Capitalism." Capitalism and the ethic anchored in the religion on which our Nation is founded – merge in synergy. This merger results in what some can see as "elements of socialism." Take away our religion, supplant it with atheism (or some ancient foreign doctrine of an eye-for-an-eye or the revengeful, unforgiving, merciless Quran) and you will take away our ethical and moral core! I do not need to go to church every day and pray in a pew in order to stand on firm moral ground, but I also cannot deny that religion and belief in God (albeit in my own way) has not contributed to my ethical wealth.

Every social system has its supporting religion. The religion of socialism is the state, its God is the Government. Make of it what you will, but do not confuse socialism and what democrats (mistakenly, albeit technically correctly) refer to as a "social democracy." There is a difference between what is technically correct (that is transmitted in technical English to the initiated group of students at a political science course) and what is said and understood by the common man, who would not be able to define and distinguish between a "social democrat" and a "democratic socialist." Why?

The democratic socialists took over the term "social democracy" (indeed, they kidnapped, hijacked it!) and have held it captive for so long that it has itself forgotten what it means. Western Europe is as much "socialist" as North Korea is capitalist or Iran is democratic. You cannot compare a parliamentarian multi-party democracy (please, drop the term "social" because it is misleading) and socialism. For that matter, you have to be very careful drawing parallels between this true multi-party democracy and our two-party system. Our system is unique, as is our country. Our Country is young and will never be as firmly rooted as an aristocracy, communism/socialism (totalitarian system) or hereditary monarchy.

We have evolved and overcome centralized Federalism during our birth and early years, why bring it back? Do you really want to change the Democratic Party to a socialist party? Well then, let us call it not social democracy or democratic socialism, because that is too confusing, but let's call a spade a spade: Federalist Socialists, Centralist Socialists, Communists – pick up one.

Of course, we will then have to change the name of the Republican Party to Democratic-Republican Party, better yet: Republican-Democrats, for we are all democrats in the old Greek sense of the word. Why did I have to add that? Something tells me we have been there before...

An Act of Love?

An act of love is not always an act of goodness or blessing. An act of love is not always returned by love. An act of love is not always a sign of inner power and composure.

Often, an act of love means caving under pressure. It is based on rationalization, Christian charity and social propriety. Protestant virtue accepts Christian charity. Hindu and Buddhist religions recognize love in all its many forms, including charity. Have we seen any charitable Muslims lately?

It is not an act of love to say: come on in, use my house, use me and when you have used me up, move on, because I am like Jesus. No-one is like Jesus. No-one wants to end like Jesus. The society is based on self-interest and self-reliance.

Charity is not an act of love, because giving without taking is not an act of love. Love is only love when it is reciprocal, when I love and I am loved back, when I take and I give back, give in return.

Selfless love is love which does not expect anything in return – however, it can only be called "love" so long as reciprocal love is given in return. Once there is no act of reciprocal giving, it ceases to be love – it becomes a charity.

Charity can only exist within a family, within one state, one nation, because it has to have clearly delineated and respected laws. Where the subject-taker is distant and either does not know nor respects these laws, charity must end. Such are the dictates of Mother Nature, which teaches us that self-preservation is the end-motif in the fight of the fittest.

Love is a reciprocal relationship based on both metaphysical and pragmatic mutual use. Alas, there is a fine line runs between use and abuse. Use is to the mutual benefit. Abuse is one-sided and ends in the demise of both parties: the one by being abused, the other by being self-abused.

Love and abuse often move in close proximity, sometimes intersect, as do love and charity, because a repeated, unrequited act of love constitutes a pattern, which belies the basic moral imperative: Act in such a way so as to make your act a universal law.

There can be no universal law based on continual selfless acts of love by one party toward the other where the latter is constantly taking and the former constantly giving. That is called slavery and is either a resulting consequence of, or the primal cause leading to, war.

Thus, every act of love conceals within itself the potential for becoming an act of war. Such war need not be provoked. It may, and often is, merely the result of a pre-emptive strike produced by the urge for self-preservation. The only way to prevent an act of love turning into an act of war lies in reciprocity based on self-reliance. Teach self-reliance and thou wilt teach love.

Democracy v. Theocracy

Theocracy means the "rule of God" [*theo+cracy*]. It associates rulers and priests, requires subjugation, allows for no freedom of thought, no original thought. It produces no science but only esoteric mysteries and prophesies. It has no researchers – only augurs and prophets.

Democracy is the "rule of the people" [*demos* = people]. Modern democracy is the product of revolutions against the stale scholasticism of Catholic aristocracy and oppression of free thought. Enlightenment of the mind, equality and freedom in education and achievement are the principal features of democracy.

The problem between democracy and theocracy (or any other totalitarian regime) is that of personal relation to state authority and the function of the state versus that of the individual in society. What is of primal value and function for every theocracy is conformity and authority. In democracy, authority means administration and delegation.

While a theocracy will place a great emphasis on morals, this emphasis lies only in conformity to blind faith that the directives "from above" are divine and binding. This leads to ethical passivity. In Catholicism, forgiveness and absolution for one's sins follows only upon conformity to the theological moral decree. In true theocracies, such as Islamic Sharia, the law is based on ancient precedents (from Muhammad's times), analogy, pre-Islamic customs, and public benefit and welfare. Thus, for example, it is to the public benefit that a rapist should marry his "tainted" victim.

Public benefit is a most dangerous and least objective argument in every law. However, connected with a theocratic regime, it is lethal, fatal, destructive of every non-conforming individual. Absolutist restraint rules over all, thus even here, in a theocracy, the "public benefit" argument is only a means to the end.

What is perhaps the most destructive feature of a theocracy is its emphasis on the ancient precedent and preservation of the old (be it a law, custom, form of punishment...). Democracy, on the other hand, emphasizes the new. Democracy wants to create, humanize, make the individual the center-piece on the chessboard. The queen may fall by the action of a pawn. The king may be cornered by a knight and a horse...

Arguably, this also makes democracy fragile and sensitive to a totalitarian attack, which always comes clothed in a cape of forgiveness or with pretense and appeal at some higher "moral" ground, which is often unattainable, because only God can do so and we are supposed to imitate and approach that which we can never quite reach (e.g. "Thou shalt not covet.") Most of these moral appeals are based on conformity to the theocratic nomenclature and rule. They attack us where it hurts the most: naked black children on the T.V. screen, homeless, stateless refugees begging for food and water... These are humanitarian appeals and we never turn a deaf ear to them.

However, at the very core, you shall find the issue of ethical magnitude you never expected: the problem of authority. The authority of our world based on free thought and conduct is undermined by the burden of the past brought to us from civilizations and nations we ceased to understand two centuries ago. How long is that? Eight generations?

Democracy is the "rule of the people" and if the people chose, they may overthrow their rulers. They may even re-instate theocracy or socialism. If a sufficient number of people demand that there be conformity and stringent moral rules, although such rules crush personal ethics, it shall be so.

History moves in a spiral. Theocracy and democracy intersect where it touches the heart. However, only a democracy may choose theocracy or socialism or communism. To reinstate democracy will always be a bloody battle which only the strong and brave survive. Only those who can think freely and creatively, and covet not because God commands them so but because their healthy pride and admiration tells them not to.

All democratic ethics are personal ethics, forming an individual code, which cherishes non-conformity while respecting the other individual. All theocratic ethics means is a moral code, blind adherence to ancient rules, which have little or no respect for the individual and their creative, thoughtful mind. If found, such a mind must be expunged, eradicated, abolished, done away with. Why?

In the ancient days, the individual served the society. Survival of the village or tribe depended on total subjugation of the individual and their service to the whole.

Today, in a free democratic state, the whole is best served by personal education, progress of the mind, creative thought and high personal ethical standards. Of course, only he who has the courage and perseverance (given the freedom to cultivate such qualities) shall achieve high ethical standard and ultimately advance the whole.

The Rise of Factions:
What is "Social" – Democracy?

Guy Fawkes "anti-capitalist demonstrations" swept upon London this week. Several policemen were gravely injured and the cool, calm Englishmen challenged any and every symbol of the government in their protest to – ? – to install a more powerful socialist government which will hold a tighter grip over them and teach them manners!

Sanders' faction tells us to look up to European democracies as if they were some kind of magic bullet, a salve to all our aches. First, he says they are "social democracies," by which he means "socialist democracies" – ruled by democratic socialists. This is not true. In fact, they are representative democracies, where all major and minor factions have their own parties and are represented in the government. There are "social democrats" represented in the parliament, but they are only one of many parties. Further, they are "social democrats" not "democratic socialists" like Sanders. There is a world of difference between the two, which I explain below.

What is more, Sanders' "paragon of socialism" – Scandinavia (he uses Denmark, Norway, and Sweden as examples) – are monarchies with multiparty (6-7 parties) representation in the parliament. We, on the other hand, we have no king – as they do. We have a REPUBLIC! Our republic is a federation with two-tiered presidential election (via direct vote, and the Electoral College) and the system of independent powers (pursuant to Montesquieu's Laws), which are there to avoid the takeover by factions. It is not perfect, but it has made US what we are – the best democracy in the world!

Federalist 10 deals with the ilk of Sanders' factions. Even then, Madison was feared and misunderstood – he argued in favor of a federation, a union of self-governing states, not a strong federal government, as the anti-federalists accused him of (Lat. "foederis" – a covenant).

What is wrong with "democratic socialism" aka "social democracy?" Start with the name. As Hayek pointed out in his Fatal Conceit, "social" is a "weasel word." The Left plays tricks with language – blue means red and red means blue! What a paradox: a small conservative businessman who just wants to do his thing and make a living, the paragon of PROLETARIAT, becomes the evil money-maker! "Proletariat" = working men: by turning a "working man" into "working men" we create a MASS – individuality disappears. Ha! By depriving him of his living, you shall deprive him of the opportunity to pursue his talents and hurl him on the Road to Serfdom! Can there be a greater tyranny than depriving the individual of Pursuit of Happiness?!

"Social" is a weasel word because it maligns and maims the noun which follows it. SOCIAL is an EVIL ADJECTIVE. What is social? "May I use the restroom?" – that is social... "Social" means having personal morals, etiquette. "Social" also means being gregarious and outgoing. Where "social" refers to society at large – beware! Social justice means COLLECTIVE justice. Black Lives Matter demands SOCIAL JUSTICE, because (they claim) individual justice fails them. However, in a democracy, justice is based on the individual rule of law, on the facts of the case. "Social justice" is a term without a meaning.

Communists wanted justice for all. There was one party system and whatever law was adjudicated was based on "social justice" – meaning "what is best for the Party." Is it good for the Party to have illegal immigrant voters? Then it is socially just. Is it good for the Party to take the property from the "rich" and give it to the "poor?" Then it is socially just. Who is "poor?" A family of two with only one car and one house?

I grew up in a communist kennel, a tiny gray apartment on a shabby gray street – there were no other. Party members had a house and a Moskvich imported from Russia (Moskwich had 0.7mm solid iron body and was touted as the best of Socialist engineering and car manufacturing – you could walk over the car, roll it in a ditch, with hardly a dent). Less prominent party members had a

25

Skoda or a Trabant (a car made from cardboard). Those were the three cars people were permitted to have because the manufacturers were government approved and owned monopolies…

Everything is SOCIAL in socialism. They will tell you "social" is a good word – it means equality, being together as one (Party) fighting the evil money-hungry capitalists (i.e. anyone interested in having personal property and taking care of things their own way). All rights are "social" because they are not "personal" – you cannot have anything of your own, unless it is approved by the government. What is the ultimate result? You have less and less freedom, perhaps even without realizing it, because you lose it bit by bit, thinking: "I am doing something good, good for the society, something which is 'social' thus proper, fostering 'social justice' and 'equality'," until one day you wake up and realize that all your personal freedom is gone, you are nothing but an insignificant gray speck living in a gray house in a corner street cheering a populist demagogue who is your Idol, your Icon, your Savior – because he (or she) lets you have a little bit of this and that here and there (of course, not too much, because that would incite envy and be "anti-social").

"Inequalities are inevitable price of freedom," says Margaret Thatcher in her book Statecraft. The objective of the government should be national security and administration of a unified system of laws protecting personal freedoms and constitutional rights. Everything else (including building of roads, hospitals and schools) can and should be taken over by private sector. Be it as it may, when the government starts administering "social justice" and is more interested in "social equality" than equality before the law – such government is destructive of the people it governs, and we all know what happens to such governments in the Land of the Free the Home of the Brave.

Social democracy is simply DEMOCRACY. Democratic socialism is simply SOCIALISM. To call any democracy SOCIAL is a misnomer, because it refers to the government by the name of one of the parties – Social Democrats. It is a Social Democrat Party – NOT, as Donald

26

Trump correctly pointed out – Social "democratic" Party. Every party in a representative democracy is DEMOCRATIC, just as every democracy is SOCIAL. Likewise, I am not aware of an anti-"social" party. Every party is "social" because is congregates people. You are going to a party, a social gathering – not a "social" party. If you call a party "social" you probably do not intend – but will end up with – the very opposite: how "social" were Nazi's "Social Democrats?" Indeed, the adjective "social" is completely superfluous – unless, of course, it refers to SOCIALISM. You have to choose: either you are a democratic party or a socialist party.

Republican Party is democratic, although it is not composed of democrats. It would not occur to us to call it Republican "Socialist" Party, although it is just as "social" as the Democrats. I believe the confusion comes from the lack of proper adjective: "Democrat Party" does not sound right because "democrat" is a noun. Yet, Democratic Party is an 1824 misnomer for the Jacksonian faction of Jefferson-Madison's Democratic-Republican Party. They had been "democratic" as opposed to the British monarch and their system. They had no way of foreseeing that, in our politically correct world, the left would appropriate the word to serve their ends: "democratic" has become the means to socialist ends, much like "liberal" has been hijacked by the left to mean "social."

Who would not be confused about the meaning of "liberal" vs. "libertarian?" They are opposites with the same root – liberty. If you were "liberal" in the 19th century England, you "took liberties" with "social mores," which is to say you did something anti-social, against the proper social etiquette. "Liberal" referred to free.

Today, "liberal" means progressive and left-wing, favoring the "social" powers of the government. "Liberal democrats" sounds better than "social democrats" but: let's call a spade a spade, a hammer and sickle for what they are.

"Libertarian," on the other hand, means possessing and wielding a free will, having maximum individual powers

– liberties. Thus, the two are tugging the tightrope of liberty, each at one end, and when it tears, anarchy is born, as we have seen in London this week.

Guy Fawkes wanted to overthrow a king, in order to install another king, who would be more conservative (Catholic). He fought against the Protestant Dutch, the country where free trade flourished and from which our Forefathers had sailed on this Continent. He was libertarian in order to be liberal. He was a socialist because he wanted one strong, powerful ruler/government. One thing he was not – a democrat. He was – like Sanders – a wolf in sheep's clothing.

Everyone is a Man of Faith

"Everyone is a man of faith. The only question is what they place their faith in," said Dr. Carson. The same Dr. Carson who was twice baptized, attends churches of different denominations, prayed in the operating room, and proclaimed that a Muslim would not be suitable for president. Let us pause and look into these statements.

There is no doubt our country is undergoing a crisis of faith, which is the result of our industrious lives, lack of proper religious education (neither morals nor religion are taught at school, thus they are also neglected at home), in turn resulting in the spread of atheism, supported by government accommodating these changes by its negative attitude to all "walls" – be it walls between states, neighbors, imaginary internet walls, or the wall between religion and state.

"Everyone is a person of faith," Dr. Carson points out, but what does he mean? Are some people "of faith" by virtue of believing in their own ability and goal? Are we "of faith" by being faithful to our spouse and family? Are we "of faith" by trusting in our government? Indeed, as we look around, "of faith" may mean faithful to the party too... One could hardly distinguish between a church mass and a canvassing concentration of adherents at a public place, heaven-bent on every word from the mouth of their political favorite...

I am no expert on religion myself, but what I like about the statement Dr. Carson made is its general applicability. Of course, he meant to appeal to the ethical core of our nation: we still "trust in God" and try to do good (most of us), and even our government makes most blunders in trying to act for "general welfare," as our Founding Document prescribes. We could quote dozens of volumes on sociology, ethnology, and political science which clearly delineate that every state is supported by, if not founded on, religion. Religion provides basic moral and ethical standards, thus also forming the social framework.

Apart from faith itself, religion encourages stable family structure, work ethic, and relationships.

Thus, we could make Dr. Carson's statement even more all-embracing: Every society is based on Faith. Here, we must pause and reflect: Hinduism and Buddhism in India, Muslim religion in the Middle East, Catholicism and Protestantism in Europe and here, their minor sub-divisions and branches we call "denominations" – they are all founding principles around which societies are constructed. We cannot abolish or abrogate a religion – unless, perhaps, when we substitute it for another. As the theocracy of Iran is incompatible with all democratic principles, Dr. Carson quite clearly stated that a faithful Muslim, because he is a follower of Islam, thus also believes in inseparability of the Church and the State, cannot become President of the United States.

Unfortunately, to the extent to which religion is officially abolished, the Ten Commandments taken down, prayers made "unconstitutional" (thus somehow "un-American"), the State meddles in the affairs of the Soul (personal Faith), we approach theocracy. How? There cannot be a "nothing" in place of "God." Two options are available: the State takes the place of God (socialism, communism) or another religion takes place of the former one (Catholicism for Protestantism, as we have seen during JFK's era – or, alas and beware (!), Islam for Catholicism). Since Islam is a proselytizing, uncompromising religion of force, whose moral principles are still stuck in the Dark Ages (corporal punishment and death by stoning being state-approved doctrinal sentences), it is incompatible with our Constitution – that is the Constitution of the American Citizen!

Even those who re-interpret our Constitution and try to "equalize" rights, enlarge benefits without correspondingly expanding obligations and duties, accept people of other faiths and cultural backgrounds – even those atheistic post-post-modernist philosophers of progress – will admit that their personal "constitutions" are much more aligned with the Constitution of the United States than that of any theocracy. To them I also say: socialism is a theocracy, and you would never be allowed to be a "person of faith" – except for one: Faith in the Party and the State.

You need not be a brain surgeon to understand the dangers of faithlessness – for both the individual and the state. Sometimes, it may seem like overdoing it: praying in the operating room or standing up for values typically associated with religion. Mind you: it is not only Catholic religion which insists on a singular definition of marriage, is anti-abortion and adheres to custom. How would you fancy a president who needs to retire to the Oval office five times a day to kneel down, facing East thinking of Allah?

On Bolsheviks, Mensheviks and Factions

In the third presidential debate in Bolder, Colorado, Cruz compared Clinton to Bolsheviks. Bolsheviks (Russian: "bolshoi" = "of the majority") were the mainstream communists who arose as Social Democratic Party of Russia at the turn of the 20th century. Subsequently, when the inner party struggle began about how to change the system, whether by a violent revolution or a natural transition, the Bolsheviks changed their name to the Communist Party (of Soviet Union), because their end was immediate socialism (ultimately communism) achieved by a revolution (October 1917).

Mensheviks, although Orthodox Marxists, were a minority (Russian: "menshoi" = "smaller"). Cruz compared Sanders to Mensheviks because 1) Sanders is more orthodox than Clinton, 2) Sanders believes in a gradual change from within (Alinsky's strategy). Mensheviks believed that socialism could not be achieved in Russia due to its economic backwardness and that Russia would first have to go through a "capitalist stage" of development.

During my junior high school years, we were indoctrinated into the idea of communism as the final, most wonderful stage of social development: Lenin was a genius because he made it happen! Marx was a genius because he materialized Hegel's theoretical dialectic and phenomenology (knowledge of the "spirit/idea" rather than simply material conditions. Hegel had revolted against Descartes, Hume, Locke, Kant – the philosophers of epistemological approach, who are indirect authors of our Bill of Rights (they preceded Hegel and our Founding Fathers built on them). They also follow the line of strict moral education and family values based on duty, obligation, and punishment for failure. As a result of Hegelian-Marxist influence and political correctness, this moral credo has become increasing blurred in our society.

Hegel, however, did not discard it or oppose it without justification. In fact, he built his philosophy on it:

Hegel's "historical materialism" consists of the interpretation of the "historical materialist struggle" as the projection of the master-slave mentality, which is to say the mentality of the feudal lords and their vassals (by close analogy also applicable to the system of American slave labor). To see it as a struggle of the "haves" against the "have-nots" (as Alinsky did a century later) is a gross simplification of what Hegel had in mind.

Hegel's philosophical breakthrough is sometimes referred to as a "mythical encounter" of two conscious beings who, in order to absorb the other's consciousness, must be self-conscious first. The ultimate goal here is that of merging conscious beings. Modern-day socialists translated this into the sphere of community organizing, seeing that even the self-conscious Bolsheviks had to merge with the Mensheviks in order to achieve their common ultimate goal. In Hegelian language, this goal would be defined as uniting individuals into a crowd of followers of a certain idea ("phenomenon"). This is what Sanders did when he passed the torch to Clinton in the last democratic debate, thus uniting the two factions of the Party.

The problem of factions is a perennial problem of every political system. It is unfortunate when the factions are destructive of the system itself, if they want to overthrow the "regime" or cause a "revolution." Revolution is not a good thing because life does not develop in sudden changes. We survive because we adapt. To adapt, we need time.

Nevertheless, there will always be uprisings. Our country was born in the wake of one: Shay's rebellion in 1787 was a revolt against centralized power as well as cronyism and politicians' inattentiveness to the needs of their people. It called for change in the Articles of Confederation and significantly affected the Constitutional Convention in Philadelphia that year.

Uprisings and rebellions flourish in the environment of dissatisfaction, poverty and poor economic conditions – which is to say: after wars. Every revolution is also followed by a short period of euphoria after which the "low" sets in: aha, life is life and grass is always greener on the other side.

Uprisings are created by factions, people united behind a common purpose, adverse to the currently prevailing system.

Madison (in Federalist 10) based his argument on the fact that the United States will be a large country governed by representative democracy. Only in the direct democracy can factions prevail, says Madison. Our political system has thus built-in precautions against being overtaken by a faction: a combination of direct and representative vote (Congress is voted directly, Presidential elections consist of popular and electorate votes), the system of checks and balances (adopted from Montesquieu) and Constitutional emphasis on the rights for life, liberty and the pursuit of happiness (taken from Locke, who emphasizes that happiness is derived from property acquired by labor).

Clearly, the change from "property" to "happiness" is not insignificant, in particular in view of the fact that factions are product of economic inequality. The aim, however, is not equality but justice. Justice, equality, and fairness are completely different notions and must never be equated. What is identical is the ultimate goal – envisioned by Madison, adopted by Locke, based on the philosophers of Scottish Enlightenment, mainly Shaftesbury and Hutcheson (Chair of Moral Philosophy at the University of Glasgow during Ben Franklin's formative years) – which is the goal of achieving the maximum general welfare.

It is no secret that Hutcheson foreshadowed Jeremy Bentham and J.S. Mill and that the argument of general welfare forms an indelible part of our legal system today, only we call it "public policy." In law school, students are told: always argue public policy. A faction revolting against the system would have them argue "politics" instead, because once the faction is formed, the individual value (the value of each individual in the crowd) dissipates and their self-identity vanishes, is given over to the ideal of the faction, be it a symbol, icon, ultimate goal in the form of revolt or revolution.

The problem with factions is fundamentally ethical and moral. All our actions are based on self-interest and self-love. Without self-interest and self-love we can neither interest the others nor love another, because we are emotionally empty. Only an emotionally fulfilled person can be moral. When an individual gives away his or her identity, passes it onto a crowd, their individual self-consciousness is minimized, negated, abolished. Their self-love is taken away along with their self-consciousness, which becomes (in Hegelian terms) a mere "phenomenon" – a "geist" or spirit used by Marxists to further the interests of the crowd.

It is not coincidental that Sanders broils against capitalist evils, mentioning the "ethical and moral immorality" of gains of the "one percent" where 99% are suffering. He chose the symbol of Wall Street as the enemy and rallied his faction behind it. The shield has been passed on to Mrs. Clinton in the last Democrat debate. Thus, as of today, the Hillary and the Sanders factions stand united to take down the enemy.

In 1969, Hillary Rodham spent one year interviewing Saul Alinsky and wrote a 92-page senior thesis on him. In 1993, White House requested that the thesis be sealed. Only a few facts are available, indicating that she was not in full agreement with Alinsky at the time it was written because Alinsky's "power/conflict model" was "inapplicable" and "anachronistic." She must have conducted serious Marxist-Leninist research into the subject to receive an "A" and be widely praised for the thesis by her professors. Nonetheless, we may only surmise at what she thinks about the subject now. Cruz's remark about Bolsheviks and Mensheviks may have rung a bell...

For us, it is important to realize that this fairly innocuous "by the way" allusion has historical implications which date back almost exactly 100 years. Only now, it is the United States, not Soviet Union, which faces the dangers of factions. I have no doubt that our system, the strongest in the world, built on minds that preceded and still overshadow such great philosophers as Hegel, Husserl, and Marx, will only become stronger by going through a crisis. Let us not forget that Russia was a feudal country ruled by a Czar, drowning in corruption, without any Bill of Rights or written Constitution at the time of its collapse... Nonetheless, thank you, Senator Cruz, for reminding us of history. It is never too late to learn more and become better!

Socialism in America

Most of what has been written on this topic concerns the United States after the foundation of the Social Democratic Party (SDP) in 1897 by a group of Marxist journalists and trade union activists (community organizers). In 1901 the SDP merged with Socialist Labor Party to form the Socialist Party of America, which gained prominence especially during the 1920s, the period of First Red Scare, followed by the candidacy of Eugene Debs for President in 1920.

Notably, Eugene Debs was in prison at the time of his candidacy for participating in violent Mayday riots in Cleveland, OH, where anarchists, communists, socialists and unionists joined to "celebrate" the Haymarket riot. The history of socialism is the history of riots and revolutions, anarchy, unions and community organizing. This powerful visceral force is the untamed devil dormant in most of us. Only hard work, drill, good habits and goal-orientation can tame it. Nonetheless, as I explain below, it has always been part of our American Psyche. The fact that Debs had been in prison multiple times by the time he ran for President, and was called a "traitor to his country" by President Wilson, yet won nearly 1mil votes, clearly points at the power of socialism in America.

Where did all this come from? Debs himself started as a unionist and member of the Democrat Party. It was not until after the infamous Pullman strike in 1893, while in prison, that he read Marx. On July 9, 1894, the New York Times editorial called Debs a "lawbreaker at large, enemy to the human race." The Communist Manifesto by Karl Marx was not published in the United States until 1872. It had been written years earlier, in 1848, during and consequent to the 1848 revolutions throughout Europe. Marx was in Brussels, penniless, ranting against greedy capitalists...

However, prior to the 1870s, socialism in America had been different and unlike its European counterpart. Socialism existed here before Marx in the form of utopian socialist communities such as New Harmony, founded in

Indiana by Robert Owen. The fact that Owen was a Welsh immigrant with several trades (saddler, iron monger, draper, eventually a mill owner in Scotland) indicates that his concept of "socialism" was that of a community engaging in work and trade. He would not have seen any difference between a "socialist" and a small businessman.

Owen was also very inventive and came up with a "truck system" of payment, wherein the company issued "tokens" and the workers could purchase goods for tokens in a company store. This system was soon abolished by the Token Acts, but it remained dormant elsewhere and would be practiced later, on a much larger scale, by the Soviet communists in the countries they would subjugate, such as Romania, where one could purchase goods only for such tokens (unless you had some West German Marks and access to the black market...).

Interestingly, Owen was supported (both ideologically and financially) by Jeremy Bentham, the founder of Utilitarianism, the doctrine whose concise motto is that "the greatest happiness to the greatest number should be the measure of right or wrong." What is more, Bentham's *Fragment on Government* coincides with our *Declaration of Independence*, wherein Jefferson famously changed Locke's "life, liberty, and the pursuit of property" to the "pursuit of happiness." Jefferson also resourced George Mason's Virginia Declaration of Rights, which restated Locke as "...life, liberty, with the means of acquiring and possessing property, and pursuing and obtaining happiness and safety."

Both Mason and Jefferson mention happiness, but Jefferson omitted entirely the idea that it is based on the pursuit of personal property. Happiness as such is an abstract idea which can be interpreted in as many ways as there are human beings on Earth. To unify this definition, communists (so called "democratic socialists") build on Bentham's utilitarianism, while capitalists (republicans) tend toward pragmatism. Practically speaking, as Bentham is largely considered the founder of modern welfare state, we may conclude that the founding stone of socialism had been laid by Jefferson in our key founding document.

Nonetheless, how it would be interpreted was unclear. Owen's "utopian socialism" was largely understood as small community utilitarianism. It was fully compatible with Emerson's and Thoreau's Transcendentalism, which stemmed from the reconciliation of Locke's empiricism with Christianity, in particular in view of the popularity of (and in opposition to) Hume's skepticism (which claimed that God is unknowable and His existence cannot be proved). Thus, two "types" of socialism were extant at this time, and ever since, in the United States: the Fourier-like anti-trade communitarianism (soon to be transformed into communism), and what we might refer to as the Transcendental "universalism.". The latter was closely tied to British romanticism: the tendency to become one with Nature, God, Universal Being – so skillfully portrayed in Whitman's Leaves of Grass and Emerson's Essays.

The fact that Transcendental universalism has always been predominant in the United States leads us to conclude that Jefferson's "pursuit of happiness" should properly be interpreted not as a socialist aspiration with communist ends but, rather, as a statement of romanticism grounded in our American admiration for Nature, the raw wilderness which sustained us from the very start and in which we were bound to live and survive. As it was impossible to survive without trade, killing, sustenance of culture upon the produce of the land... we discover there is a direct link between Jeffersonian democracy, Emerson's Transcendentalism, and universalist pragmatism of the Metaphysical Club. Trade and personal achievement have always been key to our survival and our happiness. What is more, our religious tolerance is extremely akin to Buddhist and Hinduist doctrines of nirvana and pacifism. Non-interventionism and isolationism are thus typical capitalist values: mind your business and let everyone else mind theirs!

On the other hand, revolution and anarchy is the product of communism, which fosters big government and welfare state. Reliance on government and welfare state were furthered by the likes of Debs who transformed Owen's utopian socialism into uncompromising Marxist hell. As indicated above, Owen's philosophy stems from Bentham's utilitarianism and is closely tied to Hume's skepticism. This means that socialist understanding of the "pursuit of happiness" is directly opposed to and antithetical to the "pursuit of happiness" in the vein of Jefferson, Emerson, Peirce, Holmes and William James. It is anti-Christian and anti-individualistic. It hates every Donald Trump and Steve Jobs. It admires big, totalitarian do-gooders, wolves in sheep clothing whose mottoes are: there is safety in numbers; proletariat unite; forget about the individual – think about the mass! This type of socialism is skeptical, communitarian and revolutionary. It understands well the strict, Sharia-Muslim organized tyranny, because it is one.

In conclusion, the American transcendental "socialist" philosophy starts in 1800 with Jefferson's extolling the soil and culminates in 1900 with William James' "functional psychology." The Marxist line of socialist communism in America starts with Robert Owen and culminates with Eugene Debs. The twentieth century socialism from the First Red Scare to the Second Red Scare to Alinsky, Clinton and Sanders must be viewed as a restless dweller in our republic's cellar. From time to time, the old, disheveled ghost will emerge to point at the "evil Wall Street" crying wolf. This idling Socialist will inevitably climb upstairs to denigrate all our fundamental values: industriousness, self-reliance, independence, personal and national pride. He will preach political correctness – attacking our language, our faith, our culture of pragmatism and personal property. Socialists' most powerful vehicle is ENVY. Envy is moral because it is justified by fairness. Violence is moral on the same grounds... Are we going to need new Espionage and Sedition Acts to deal with these anarchists?

Finally, it must be emphasized that transparent democracy means republican system of accountability. It is good for us to see who they are and what they want. Let us

40

help them out of the cellar. Let us lead them to the light of day. Let us show them the mirror of their likeness. They (Sanders and his sheep) have grown up in the best country in the world, benefitted from all the advantages of capitalism – only to turn into shiftless monsters of socialism!

It was under F.D.R. that socialists were Prompted to join Democrats. Prominent Democrats, such as David Dubinsky, called upon Socialists to vote Democrat in 1936 – and have done so ever since. Socialists' ranks shrunk, until they fell below 2,000 during the McCarthy Era. Socialists crawled into capitalist cellars again, awaiting the opportunity, which came with the Civil Rights Movement. They hijacked the cause and lulled the black people. It is easy to appeal to the primeval instincts in us all: envy and propensity to violence. Finally, 1968, the Socialist Party of America came up with a presidential candidate – Hubert Humphrey. Four years later, in 1972, it was George McGovern. In those years, while Donald Trump was building and renovating housing complexes in New York and Ohio, Sanders and Clinton joined the New Left and began their careers of community organizing. Eugene Debs and Karl Marx would be proud of them.

What is a "Single Payer Healthcare" system?

Like most of you, I have recently had the misfortune of losing my health insurance due to Obamacare. After "shopping around" for a significant period of time, I opted for a PPO "bronze plan" with $240/month payments – no dental and no vision, as I had previously had with my employer. I am paying three times as much, receiving less than one half of the services. Thank God, I do not need them, but – one never knows.

Perhaps, there was good will at the start of this healthcare reform, but it is all built on empty promises and wishful thoughts. I have noticed some left-wing arguments on social media vociferously asserting that "more socialism" is needed in our country and that until we have a One Payer System, our Healthcare will not be satisfactory. Most of them probably do not understand that such a system means that all responsibility for your health is passed on to the government, which constitutes the Single Payer. In other words: you pay whether you want it or not and you get what the government deems you deserve, no more.

Single Payer System is the first step to socialist medicine. Its proponents argue that it is needed because of preventive care – in other words, people do not know how to take care of themselves, they overeat, smoke, use drugs... then end up in the hospital without healthcare. According to some estimates, there were 50mil people uninsured in 2009, out of whom 50% had personal income over $50,000 and could very well have afforded insurance. Hence, Obamacare consitutes the decision to force a standard plan insurance one-fits-all type on all of us. It is not the Single Payer System yet, but close enough.

We all know that prevention is better than cure and many diseases and even deaths can be prevented by better care: from washing hands to improved dietary habits. I grew up in socialism where there was a Single Payer System. A doctor came to school, children lined up, everyone received a shot in the shoulder, everyone had to take Fluoride pills distributed by the teacher, everyone had to go to the dentist's office. My mother had told me once, "Don't let them pull any teeth!" When the dentist was going to pull my tooth, I ran away, came home from school early – and was in trouble, of course. Visiting a dentist was counted as "school hours" so I was de facto absent from school without excuse. Moreover, I refused to have my tooth pulled! Who has ever heard of that?! A "B" in morals was suggested. My mother had to visit with the Principal and apologize. "But there's nothing wrong with my tooth," I said, "it's perfectly healthy!" Well, the government knew better. I saved my tooth – but was branded forever after as a "trouble-maker."

When you are sick in a Single Payer System, you have one physician you must see: one for ENT, one internist, one podiatrist... I used to suffer from sore throats and flus a lot. We would go to the doctor's office, wait for hours in a packed waiting room full of coughing and sneezing people, then a rough lady-doctor in a swivel chair with that funny mirror in the middle of the forehead would look at me: "say: AAHHH!" and then she would use one thin needle-like instrument wrapped in cotton, plunge it into some dark, sour liquid and shove it several times down my throat till I gagged. "Next one!" she'd call. Of course, once we began to bring wine and chocolates, we waited only for an hour, not three or four hours, but still. Bribes were necessary, because everyone was paid the same and had the same insurance and was to receive the same treatment. Did it help? Yes, but it was so unpleasant... I could not understand why they wouldn't just sell that liquid and we could "treat" ourselves at home. Oh, well, that was a Single Payer System, not a Choose Yourself or Do It Yourself one. I will never forget the doctor and I will never forget the stares of other people in the waiting room when we received a "preferential treatment." You see, it was unusual for a non-Party member like my mother to receive any "extra" treatment...

So people want more "socialism" in the United States? Maybe they should go to Cuba and try out their Single Payer System for a couple of months. Some HillBills and ClintBamas out there assume that more government will solve their problems – because, after all, they are bigger and have "resources." More government leads to one thing only: more spending! More government is always less effective and costs more. The best healthcare is: private healthcare for serious diseases only (competition among private insurance companies), ordinary things (regular checkups) paid for from your own pocket, and good prevention (healthy lifestyle). Government preventive care is an oxymoron, because government never prevents anything – and rarely fixes something so that it works.

Next, hospitals charge too much, which triggers high insurance premiums and high co-pay. It is a vicious circle but so long as the average cost of appendectomy is $33,000 and giving birth is $10,000, how can insurance companies cope? Can the government? The next step would be to nationalize all healthcare and hospitals – a true socialist system. Compare that to small outpatient surgery centers that compete for major surgeries, such as liposuction or facelift for under $5,000!

Of course, a tort reform is needed. I have recently come up against a large LA hospital that called a small army of attorneys to the table and did not hesitate to pay their testifying experts $750/hr. – no questions; and, yes, no great answers either... Naturally, neither the lawyers nor the experts cared about time – after all, they were all paid by the insurance company! However, as the other sides works on contingency, the insurance company ultimately pays for litigation of both parties, provided that the plaintiff prevails. The insurance company cannot lose because no matter who wins, they pay – it may be a little less if the defense wins, but: "Hey, who cares – we'll raise the premiums!"

Ultimately, the quality of any "system" boils down to the quality of the individual. If you are made of marble, diamond, titanium, if your morals are strong and ethics supported by your faith, if you act conscientiously to yourself as well as others, society can rely on you – but, what is more, you can rely on yourself! If not, you are just a stone anyone can kick around at their pleasure.

Unfit for President

While Hillary Clinton was writing her grand thesis on Alinsky, and Sanders was organizing protests in Chicago, Donald Trump took on his first great project, to revamp the foreclosed Swifton Village apartment complex in Cincinnati, OH, a 1,200-unit complex, which he turned from 34% to 100% occupancy. He subsequently sold it at a profit, for $6.74mil!

In 1971, Trump moved to Manhattan with the same idea in mind – to improve housing for the middle class. He purchased decrepit and dilapidated buildings around Brooklyn, Long Island, even Manhattan – and made them top-notch again. This aroused the attention of the government, of which Clinton was already an indelible part, as we shall see below. In 1973, he was accused by the Justice Department of violations of the Fair Housing Act in the operation of 39 buildings. What were the charges? Trump was accused of refusing to rent to welfare recipients, mostly those who were likely to damage the properties and not pay any rent. Thus, he was treated as an anti-minority, anti-government rebel! We can only imagine how difficult and costly it must have been to rebut such charges… (which he successfully did in 1975).

Interestingly, by then, Hillary Rodham had enrolled at the super-white-privileged Yale, and started lawyering on the opposite side of the scales, prosecuting landlords who refused to rent to welfare recipients. In 1970, one year before she started dating Bill Clinton (also a Yale student), she was awarded a grant to work at Marian Wright Edelman's Washington Research Project, where she was assigned to Senator Walter Mondale's Subcommittee on Migratory Labor. (Marian Wright was an African-American "activist" who met Mr. Edelman four years earlier when Edelman was a supporting staff member of Robert Kennedy's "entourage" when the latter was visiting southern slums.)

Incentivized by Marian Edelman, Rodham was viscerally involved in providing penurious immigrants, often illegal, with housing, sanitation, health and education. She was paid for by the government and stood for the government and regulations against private entrepreneurs like Donald Trump.

It should be of general interest to us that the current left-wing establishment had largely been formed in the early 1970s. Mondale's Subcommittee on Migratory Labor members included, by means of example, the following:

- Community organizer of Polish descent Barbara Mikulski: with BA in social sciences, she never held a job, and is currently the longest serving female member of Congress (longer than I have been alive, and I am no spring chicken anymore…!)
- Community organizer of Polish descent (also the first generation Pole, like Mikulski), Bernie Sanders, admirer of Hitler and Marx, whose only degree is also a BA (political science)
- Patty Murray, a "citizen-lobbyist" from Brooklyn, whose only qualification for 30 years in Senate (apart from community organizing) is a BA in physical education. Murray described herself as a "mum in tennis shoes…"

Shall I go on?

- Al Franken, the "improvisational comedian" (Al Franken Show) who likes political satire and whose only qualification is a BA in "government." I did not even know you can study and major in "government." How does that prepare you to be a productive member of our society?

Enough, please.

All right, so how about the man allegedly "unfit for presidency" Donald Trump? He earned his BA in economics from Wharton and immediately began to work in his father's firm, improving living conditions for the middle class. He took a loan $1mil and made it $1bil! Who can do that?! It is like making one dollar into a million!

Not many people also know that Trump was always a maverick, filled with healthy self-love and ego which I call American Pride. To "restrain" him, his father enrolled him in the New York Military Academy (NYMA), where he attained the rank of captain.

Does Clinton have a better qualification to be our Commander-in-Chief? Who is she again? A kowtowing pawn of a Secretary of State who hides e-mails and lies to everyone, probably including herself...

They are accusing Donald Trump of going through bankruptcy, which only shows ignorance of law – Chapter 11 bankruptcy serves to rearrange debt payments and enable a struggling business to make profit. No wonder it is politicians, who have never worked or run a business, who accuse Trump of failing because he pushed a casino through bankruptcy!

However, Donald Trump came to the rescue of many more businesses than we can imagine, large and small. He took on the burden of many foreclosed and bankrupted real estate deals and made them into successful enterprises. The Cincinnati complex in Ohio is one such example. Even more famously, he had an option to buy and made plans to develop the Penn Central Transportation Company, which was in bankruptcy. This venture included the 60th Street rail yard on the Hudson River (Riverside South) and the Grand Central Terminal, for which he paid $60 million. He turned the bankrupt Commodore Hotel next to Grand Central into the Grand Hyatt and created The Trump Organization, employing thousands of people and doing more for the poor, unemployed and immigrants seeking labor than any "community organizer in-chief" could ever dream of!

Let us also underscore that these projects required the government to get out of the way. For example, the repairs on the Wollman Rink in Central Park, built in 1955, had begun in 1980 with an expected 2 1⁄2-year construction schedule, but were not completed by 1986. Trump took over the management of the project without any city subsidy and completed it in three months for $1.95 million, which was $750,000 less than the initial budget! Whenever I see the scaffolding around the Congressional dome, I think of Donald Trump...

Communism says money is evil. All that the Big Government and socialist "redistribution" can produce is envy and more poverty! As John Stossel pointed out, in spite of the left-wing Democrat propaganda, world poverty levels are approximately one half of what they had been twenty years ago. US poverty stagnates between 10-20%, with single family households about twice as much. Why? Think about $160bil we gave to Iran or the billions in foreign aid and UN support... Notably, however, our citizens spend approximately the same regardless of how much they make, which means that the more people have, the more they value what they have.

Capitalism is not about having but about doing – the very opposite of communism! For us, capitalists, money is the byproduct of our work. Other people's money is the source of inspiration and excitement – leading to healthy competition, not envy. We strive harder, because life is a race and only the strong ones survive – not the sheep on social support, not the envy-ridden community organizers with little knowledge and even less scruples, whose sole aim is to rule over others and have more, not do more.

Let us ask ourselves again who is the one truly "unfit for president." Is it the one who preaches welfare and redistribution, organizes and sucks up to the ignorant – or the one who practices, does, enlightens and proves himself by the fruits of his labor?

The Lure of Sugar Daddy Sanders

According to the latest survey, 84% of people under 35 want to vote for Sanders. Does this mean that 84% of young Americans want socialism? When I listen to Sanders, he has no concrete plan. All he wants is to "tax Wall Street speculation to pay for college" and increase taxes to 90% with respect to everyone else.

What does it mean "Wall Street speculation?" He wants to take any and all profit you may make as an investor purchasing and selling shares. He wants the government to be the final judge and arbiter as to which business should succeed and which fail. While most banks do not give any interest to those who want to save (mine gives 0.1%!), one can make 2-5% in investing in stocks and bonds. This will not be permissible under Sanders. What is more, Sanders completely abolishes all theories of the value of money (Locke, Adam Smith, Ricardo), as I explain below.

Socialism requires a centralized economy, not a competitive market but economy directed by the Politburo (DNC), which will take away money from oil companies in order to finance Solydra etc. The next step is allowance of property, let us say: no single family shall be permitted to own a house worth more than $1mil... Schools will be for free but no matter how hard you study, you will not be any more eligible for university unless both your parents are significant contributors to the DNC. Of course, if they are, you will be an Ivy League, no matter what your results. In the end, such a person may become a doctor, surgeon, lawyer... and kill your mother on the table or sentence an innocent man to death. Lawsuits? You cannot sue an honorable Party member – ever! At best, the judge will say: "What difference – at this point – does it make?" At worst, you will end in jail yourself. Why, you virtually tried to sue the Party itself!

I could go on and on, because that is the environment in which I grew up and still remember – only too well. However, let me explain what underscores Sanders' popularity and this repetitive rise of communism in

49

our country (for we had had it in 1918 and then again during McCarthy era). First, Sanders is an old man who promises the young, naïve, gullible sheep blue from the sky. The comparison I heard Greg Guftfeld make to Santa Claus is arrogate. Young people who have not had to work or have not experienced the natural forces of the market feel only needs that crave to be satisfied. Such satisfaction must come from without – and who else should be the bearer of good news than an old sugar daddy with gray hair and a good-natured smile!

What is more important, we all know that Thomas Jefferson was well read and one of the chief sources of the Declaration of Independence was John Locke's Second Treatise on Government. Jefferson probably took more from George Mason's Virginia Constitution, which incorporated a similarly worded Declaration of Rights, but he must have known that John Locke's Treatises constituted a powerful rebuttal to the absolutist paternalism of Sir Robert Filmer and the benevolent surrender to totalitarianism in the skeptical Leviathan of Thomas Hobbes. Such works propounded and supported the absolute monarch as a patriarch and viewed the whole society as a family, status quo headed by the alpha male, descendant of Adam, at whose benevolent, merciful feet we should kowtow, pay our tithes and worship him till death. No wonder modern socialists do not see Muslims as evil because Sharia is very much in accord with such views...

Our country is based on the rights to life, liberty and the pursuit of happiness, derived from such magnificent thinkers as Locke, Voltaire, Rousseau, and the philosophers of the Scottish Enlightenment: Francis Hutcheson, David Hume, Adam Smith, Thomas Reid, Adam Ferguson and others. The pursuit of happiness was re-phrased by Mason. Originally, Lock spoke of the "pursuit of property" in the sense of following the acquired value: if I take possession of public land and irrigate it, improve it, use it for others' (and my own) benefit (e.g. by growing wheat), such land acquired value through my labor, the excess of labor is mine and I am free to sell it, market it etc. By the same token, I have taken possession of the land, tilled it and built upon it – the land becomes mine through my actions. Adam Smith's theory of Invisible Hand of the market is based on this rationale.

Of course, property is a word of far-reaching implications and connotations. Socialists would like us to think of money, always money – in terms of the rich vs. the poor, the haves and the have-nots – not in terms of those who work and those who idle. Paradoxically, it was Marx who pointed out that alienation of labor, introduced by Smith and Locke, is tantamount to "alienation of selfhood." By adding value, one adds a part of one's self, one's own soul – to property (as Marx said in Das Kapital). So far, Locke and Marx would be in agreement. It was the next sadomasochistic step that turned tables on Locke: everything in the world consists of an abstract "value" which is a part of some larger ideology, which has been misappropriated and abused by the "evil capitalist" who, in exploiting the concrete market value of a commodity, is in fact exploiting the abstract identity of the proletariat (workforce). While there may have been some justification for this rationale 150 years ago, it is hardly the case today.

Instead of taking Marx as a significant step forward in terms of spreading personal liberty, i.e. the world is more free, not less, when the market trades in goods that have acquired our rights and values (indeed our personal and national pride), the socialists took Marx's criticism of capitalism as a guide to appropriating the power to rule over people by taking the value each person has added to commodity/property, abolishing free market, and creating a system of paternalistic hierarchy within ideology – ideology, which Marx defined as interests uniting a particular "social class." Thus, Railroad Labor Unions would be united by their interest in railroads because the workers have contributed their (personal) value to the product (rails, locomotives, upkeep, etc.). Since the followers of Sanders have little and produce little, they are identified by the ideology of the evil "speculator," some mythical rich man who has mafia-like lackeys on the stock exchange and spends 5 months in Florida, 5 in Hawaii and 2 in New York. What unites them is not their added value but the envy of someone else's added value – which would be sad, but is in fact absurd, because such value is imaginary.

As Alinsky clearly delineates in the Rules for Radicals, people are not ruled by money but by their desires, wants and suffering. Marxist socialism stands market theory of value on its head: people must not freely trade in the added values but shall be ruled by them from above. Marx assumed this was what capitalists did to proletariat, so, read between the lines: the time has come for revenge. It should also be noted that anyone could run a business or enterprise in England or the United States at the time. Napoleon scornfully declared that England was a "nation of small shopkeepers." Think of yourself: we all love to show off our value, the product of our work, which is more than some gadget, trinket or piece of writing… but a product of our heart and soul. There is more satisfaction and pleasure in that than any pleasure derived simply from money. Money is a byproduct.

Not so for a socialist. For a socialist, money is a means of manipulation of a social class. Every ideology is a half-truth (as Marx stated) because people are required to suspend their disbelief. Sanders says: "I'll tax Wall Street speculation and thus I'll pay for your college." Thus, he unites the young under the false belief that their college will be paid for by someone else. Their parents are happy too, of course – unless they can see through the thin veneer of the word "speculation."

All market is speculation. When I go shopping, I speculate whether turkey or chicken is better or if I should buy this type of milk rather than the other one: I look at price, contents… That is exactly what Wall Street "speculators" do. That is also what the store owner does when he is ordering the goods – looking at how much of what item has been sold. You cannot "tax speculation" without harming the market, which ultimately harms you, because this eliminates choice, bankrupts companies, drives people out of work. Such people will have one thing in common – suffering.

Marx famously said that "religion is the opium of mankind." Many people know this, but not many people realize the insight of his psychology: Marx spoke about ideology and gave religion as an example. What he meant to say is that people will suffer and long for absolution. You cannot take away their suffering, because you would take away the absolution. Thus, religion is indispensable. Communists made the state indispensable by the same rationale. All socialists are communists. All communists are sadists – they want you to suffer, not themselves. Every socialism develops a "privileged class" of Party members and more privileged Party members. "All animals are equal – but some are more equal than others..." that is what Sanders' smile says, never mind his words. The psychology is too sophisticate to see through by a modern teenager brought up in the Land of Plenty. It took me years of suffering and self-education to be able to recognize this Evil – and I am probably inoculated to it only because I had had to experience it first hand.

Who Is Sanders?

Bernard Sanders grew up in Brooklyn in an orthodox Jewish family, attended a Hebrew school, later studied at Brooklyn College and transferred to Chicago University for a BA in Political Science, his only degree. He attributes his "mediocrity" to lack of interest in studies, because he wanted to be more involved in community organizing, going out, not staying home with books. Another reason? He admired Hitler, as he says, for the power Hitler had over people. He was fascinated with this power and always wanted to follow a political career leading to such a position.

As a Young Socialist (member of the Socialist Party of America) he organized the first Chicago sit-in, protested housing discrimination, and marched on Washington in 1963 to hear Martin Luther King in person. Of course, he met Saul Alinsky and Noam Chomsky, even before he ran as a Democrat for Mayor of Burlington. No-one ran against him on the Republican side... He was a good mayor, they say, improving all public areas, making everything he could public: park, science center, embankment, housing...

You can do that with a small town or even a small country, such as Denmark (population 5mil.), not with a country the size of the United States! Why? We want the individual to have the power. The power of each of us rests in how capable we are, how hard we work, what we earn and reinvest of our own volition. In short, private property equals freedom. Take away property, collectivize it, you have a nation of slaves.

Of course, socialism is based on abolition of private property and government distribution of your labor, your healthcare, and all freedoms and rights. Socialism is only a transitory stage to communism, as defined by Marx and Engels in their Communist Manifesto in 1848. Interestingly, community organizing and public speaking are foundations of the "rule from above," which lies at the core of socialism: economy is planned, directed, by the Party apparatchiks. Politics are based on economy!

When Sanders says all he wants is "democratic socialism," he is misleading his followers. There is no such thing as "democratic socialism!" Denmark and Sweden are parliamentary representative democracies, fundamentally republics with multiparty parliamentary representation. No-one there calls them "socialist."

What is more, as a member of Socialist Youth and Socialist Party of America, Sanders knows only too well that Marx adopted his idea of accrued property value from Locke, who defined the product of labor as accrued value, part of the individual producing the item which the individual puts on the market, either as a service or a good. Locke's theses (First and Second Treatise on Government) were rebuttals of Sir Robert Filmer's Patriarch and Hobbes' Leviathan, works which confirmed the patriarchal system of government, subservience to the king (note, for example, that all legislature in Denmark must still be approved by the King).

Marx turned Locke against him when he stated: let us take back the accrued value (taken away by the evil capitalists) and let the "proletariat of the world unite!" This thought leads to the abolishing of free market economy (tax Wall Street till there is no Wall Street) and obliterating of the state as an entity: true communism is borderless - the world must unite as one proletariat.

Thus, Marxism is very similar to radical Islamism. Some of the arguments are rational, but not realizable - unless the end is total subjugation and tyranny, which always ends in tyrant's death and a new bloody revolution... Please stop calling for a revolution! We must understand that a utopia is called "utopia" for a reason. All such idealistic progressive thoughts date back to Plato's Republic and Thomas More's Utopia (1516). Utopia means "ou-topos" (Gk. "no place") and "eu-topos" (Gk. "good place"). No place is a good place - for a communist-socialist ideologue.

Whichever tail of the coat of socialism you grasp, be it economy or social polity without borders, it is not realizable in practice: whenever socialism arose, as I personally witnessed, it destroyed the individual, resulted in corruption and fear, and marred several subsequent generations of people.

It should be noted that socialism is founded on mediocrity – which is probably why Sanders has always viewed mediocrity as positive, dedicating himself to the "life of the community," as he said, not to studies. After all, mediocre people are easy to subjugate – they have little personal aspiration beyond food and shelter, and – more importantly – ignorant of everything else, they are easy to indoctrinate. Sometimes, as was the case with Sanders, self-indoctrinate...

Having been in Congress since 1991, Sanders is an ultimate insider. Yet, his only education is a BA in political science. His wife, Jane O'Meara, is a community organizer (BA in social work) with a doctorate in "leadership studies" from Union Institute (experimental, distance-learning "university" founded in 1964, which went bankrupt and was disbanded in 1982, then revamped, later purchasing Vermont College from Norwich University, VT). Today, the ultra-liberal descendant of the Union Institute offers Ph.D. in "interdisciplinary studies." Is this how we want to educate our youth?!

Finally, Jane Sanders O'Meara was a social worker and community organizer in Burlington, where Sanders was Mayor. She became President of Burlington College, but had to retire in 4 years, fired for causing "a toxic and disruptive environment." Her salary was $160K, severance pay $200K. Today, Jane Sanders O'Meara is the one who decides everything regarding Sanders' policy and appearances. As he says, she is "one of his key advisors, administrative & policy adviser, chief of staff and media buyer" and, interestingly, Sanders credited her with drafting more than 50 pieces of "his" Congressional legislature.

Shall we vet our candidates or stay complacent and elect another puppet in the hands of political hacks and ideologues - this time the one who looks up to Hitler and Marx as paragons of political power?!

When Did We Start Looking Up to Europe?!

When did we start looking up to Europe as an example of how we should govern and what our state and federal organization should be? How little do those that cite the examples of Denmark and Sweden know about those countries... Both are monarchies, both are governed from Brussels. Corporate income tax in Denmark is 23%, Sweden 22%; personal income tax 30-47% and 59% maximum respectively – which is a far cry from Sanders' 90% tax. How much would you take home from a $15/hour wage under Sanders' administration...?

Those who denounce and decry ideology the most, are those who are most likely to espouse it. During the 2009 elections, Sen. Obama was asked if he would still raise taxes on "the rich" even if he knew (not thought or surmised, but if it were a proven fact) that such a raise would hurt our economy. "I'd consider it," he said. That is ideological blindness.

Now think Sanders would say! He preaches to us of "morality." In the New Left PC of this socialist ideologue to be moral means to be revengeful. "We must raise taxes on the rich," he says, not because it will help the economy but "because it is moral and the right thing to do." Each new "social democrat" moves further left, becomes a "democratic socialist," until he or she drops the word "democratic" altogether.

Thus, Denmark and Sweden are not the ends he aspires to become – they are the means, stepping stones for his ideology. He does not want to stop with Denmark and Sweden – he wants the Soviet Union of the 1970s and 1980s. Collectivization, five-year plans and the rule of the Party Dictate – those are his ultimate ends. Denmark and Sweden? He probably just looked them up on Wikipedia as the states with the highest tax rates. Why not Poland, Slovakia, Czech Republic (where, by the way, maximum personal tax rate is 30% but it can also be zero, and maximum corporate tax is 15%!). Why? Because those post-communist countries treasure liberty too much – they knew communism and shy away from all big government and the bureaucratic dictate of Brussels…

There is another point no-one seems to notice regarding the European Union. Historically, EU has been composed of nations that have arisen from a multicultural multinational environment (former Austria-Hungary) and nations that were created at the point when (after the Peace of Westphalia in 1648), state borders were established to correspond with nationalities. Thus, modern western European concept of state-nationhood was not the same as that of central and eastern Europe, where it was commonly understood that the Empire was composed of diverse nationalities. In the nineteenth century Vienna, it would have been just as common to hear German, Czech, Hungarian, Slovak, Italian…

In France, England and post-Bismarck Germany, the concept of a "nation" was identical with that of a state, thus establishing a clearly defined notion of a citizen: I am a citizen of France because I speak French and live in (the territory called) France. On the other hand, in the amalgam of Austria-Hungary, this would have been impossible, because everyone felt their own "belonging" to the local community first. This community spoke a local language and was hell-bent on preserving their cultural customs. From this small-state nationalism, "Balkanization" was born – a process of disintegration of a nation into states. Why? Because the nation never existed as a unified entity in the first place.

Consider Yugoslavia, for instance, which had been held together by Tito under his very peculiar communist dictatorship. Stalin knew he could not have done any better there, because Croatia, Serbia, Slovenia, Kosovo, and Montenegro have always been distinct communities – with peculiar diverse religious habits, often different in speech and even the alphabet! The situation in pre-war Yugoslavia was not unlike that of pre-war Iraq. The results were not the same only because European nations are civilized and their small communities are not religious tribal societies. In other words, where there is a separation between the state and the religion, the new "nation-state" can be integrated into a community of nations.

However, the proverbial American "melting pot" has never worked out for the nation-states of former Habsburg Empire. These are what Masaryk called "small nations" with their predilections and apprehensions. They are very particular about their folk customs and habits, fairy tales, religion and symbols. Language, blood and soil – such are their roots, which no power on earth can uproot. Communism tried, but failed. Capitalism only injected more pride and healthy self-esteem into these small frightful entities. This self-esteem, however, is underscored by feelings of strong nationalistic and ethnic identity. Such feelings lead to grandiose gestures and overestimation of one's abilities. They look up to the United States, trying to imitate us, while at the same time begrudging our greatness and backbiting about our "world policing patriotism."

The European "salad-bowl" system of diverse but locally coherent and unified communities is not something we treasure here in the United States. Instinctively, we know that we were molded and forged into One though the brimstone and fire of many a battle, through suffering and abnegation, war and death... and should we be dissected and severed again like Ben Franklin's proverbial snake, we would perish as One Nation under God, torn apart for the sake of the communist ideology of diversity.

Communism has one end – totalitarian rule of one Party. Everybody must think the same, be the same, shut up and toe the line. Excuse my language, but we must call a spade a spade before it hits us on the head.

Meanwhile, we suffer in silence the less obvious totality of language – political correctness, which forces us to accept the unacceptable – which is the totality of thought. Why would anyone blame someone for saying that President Obama is a Muslim or a pussy? Much worse has been said about our former presidents. To be direct, perhaps blunt, is not the same as being rude. If it quacks like a duck...

We are accused of being narrow-minded, even racist when we defy "diversity." Our accusers are giving us Europe as an examples. They are looking up to Europe through the rosy-colored glasses of Wilsonian World Order – as a monolith, an example we should follow. But what is diversity?

Diversity is the sharp bodkin pointed at our hearts – the point of the spear of the totality of political correctness! Diversity is a means to an end. Diversity is the opposite of cultural assimilation and social integration. The latter terms are used as pejoratives per se by the modern Left. Why? Because they represent US, the United States of America.

DNC chair Debbie Wasserman-Schultz stated the other day that Democrats are "proud Americans." How can you be, when you are trying to undermine the core of American democracy, install every single instrument of socialism (from One Payer System to free education, housing, social subsidies for everyone) and even your "open borders" policy is communist – because you want to keep people in, literally incentivizing them not to leave once they come, vote for the Party and worship the Regime! If our socialist "democrats" ever decide to close the border, it will be to prevent people from moving out. Trust me, I have been there before!

I am sick and tired of looking up elsewhere to what they have that we do not! Especially looking up to Europe is painful. Europe is a disaster in the making. EU is 30 years old and constantly falling apart: a referendum is Spain, Scotland, now England… no-one wants to be subject to Brussels' dictate. They have been trying to emulate US! Are the kingdoms of Sweden and Denmark so attractive to Sanders because they are kingdoms?

Clinton, Sanders,
and the Threat of Communism

Today, having won the Cold War, Balkans, Iran... capitalism has made us too complacent and unaware of what the treat of communism really means. For Clinton and Sanders alike, everything that is wrong with our society is the fault of the "system:" there is "systemic racism," "systemic incarceration" of black people, "systemic" police violence, etc. Clinton's e-mail scandal is a product of systemic hatred and a right-wing conspiracy. This "systemic suspicion" falls on anyone who is not part of the progressive movement: Why not? They must have some secret funds in an offshore account! They must be part of a larger conspiracy! "They" are not "us!"

This "us against them" is the old Marxist motto: "If you are not with us, you are against us!" Lenin, Stalin, Hitler, Brezhnev, Khrushchev and others used to say. Clinton's tepid "Trumpian" take-off "Make America Whole again" means "It's us against them" – the socialist worker against the capitalist "pig" or, as Sanders says, "the not-haves against the haves." Property envy is a fundamental building stone of socialism. Socialism is not about striving harder to be better but about destroying what the other one has in order to be equally poor. Here is a joke which used to be traded among the youth when I was growing up in socialism:

"In Germany, when your neighbor buys a sports car, you work harder so that you can buy one too. In America, you work even harder so that you buy a better one. In Russia, you wait till dark and then venture out with a sharp key to scratch the beautiful shiny metal finish on that damned car you can't afford..."

It is not a joke, it is a way of thinking – the socialist way.

Not many people know that Hillary Clinton knew Mr. Alinsky even better than Bernard Sanders did, although the latter has more in common with him personally, being of similar orthodox Jewish dissent, revolting primarily against his parents and their idiosyncratic doctrine of Jewish allegiance. Clinton spent a whole year seeing Alinsky on a weekly basis. He taught her the fundamentals of community organizing and "establishment baiting" (in Alinsky's words). In turn, she dedicated a much praised 100-page thesis on his theory of community organizing entitled "There Is Only the Fight" which, frankly, sounds very much like Hitler's "My Fight..." (*Mein Kampf*).

That is the problem with revolutionaries: they each feel they are great individuals singled out for slaughter. This is not a doom but a blessing to them: they want to be martyrs or, rather, they need to be seen as martyrs by others. Alinsky's motto is as follows: bait the establishment, provoke them, and the moment you are attacked, stand up and say you fight for the people! Hitler rose to power in the same fashion. If anyone should dare oppose you, deny the accusations and attack them on your turf!

Hillary Clinton has met her match in Bernard Sanders though, who practiced what Alinsky preached even as she was learning the ropes as Alinsky's favorite pupil. Obama and Sanders, both active Chicago community organizers, have been on par ideologically from the very start. Hillary Clinton descended to their level of thinking about people and society only upon thorough analysis and as a result of personal disappointment.

Of Welsh descent, daughter of coalminers' on her father's side, and Canadian emigres from Bristol on her mother's side, Hillary Rodham was raised in a conservative household and her first political escapades were on the Republican side. At the age of thirteen, while most of us were occupied doing homework, playing sports or plotting a date, Hillary Rodham was on the streets of Chicago helping canvass for the 1960 U.S. presidential election. Having "detected fraud" in Richard Nixon's campaign, she turned to Goldwater as a volunteer.

While Sanders has always been an aspiring communist, Hillary Clinton's socialism is rather tepid and moderate. She began to lean to the left during the Civil Rights Movement and the Vietnam War, but her mindset has never been 100% socialist. When Sanders is attacking her "qualifications" because she is supported by Wall Street and the "big money," he is doing so from the position of a left-wing communist whose ideology does not permit capitalism at all. If Wall Street was called "Red Party USA" – why, Sanders would be Clinton's closest cohort and clansman!

Every war weans a generation of isolationist "reformists" in our country. It is they who will raise the platform of socialism. Today, the post-Vietnam War socialists are paragons of virtue and teachers to post-Iraq war communists. From the Civil Rights Movement, assassinations of JFK and M.L. King, Watergate, fuel shortages, hostage crises and volatile markets... many political activists were born. Clinton and Sanders are two – out of two million, or more... Only Cold War and the ominous cloud of nuclear holocaust prevented them from coming out fully in favor of socialism. Does it have to always go so far?!

Who is George Soros?

In 1992, two years after the fall of communism, I was studying in London, saving money to be able to complete my degree from University College London. I had two jobs, studied at night and was trying to move ahead. Then came Soros.

Overnight, all my savings were wiped out – on Black Wednesday, September 16, 1992. Soros became famous, made $1billion in short-selling stocks and "broke the Bank of England." This stock manipulation has since been made illegal: it is referred to as "Abusive Naked Shortselling" and would land Soros in jail today.

Thanks to Mr. Soros's unscrupulous thievery, I had to complete my studies in London "informally," struggling for the next three years harder than ever before, eventually moving to Prague to complete my MA. Coincidentally, the degree I so much desired was the same degree, which Soros had earned in London from the same university in 1951.

How was Soros able to complete his studies in London? A female tutor of his requested a financial aid of 40,000 GBP from the Religious Society of Friends (Quakers). Needless to say, 40,000 1951 British Pounds equal about half a million of today's dollars.

Let me reiterate: the free-trading, God-fearing Christians supported Soros with half a million in return for what? Turning him into a communist pest destroying their country today… Beware of "one good turn…" as it does not always end well!

Today, Soros has become "famous" again, for his financial backing of BLM and La Raza, the Mexican anti-white KKK, which is (with Obama's blessing, if not under his express orders) sending illegals across our southern border in order to defeat Republicans in the upcoming elections.

What is more, Soros popped up on the news in connection with Donald Trump's Chicago rally. Soros is financially backing "moveon.org" – an organization of professional disrupters and welfare sponges.

Soros is like a bad-smelling egg which I had tasted years ago and the odor has never gone away. Who is this Hungarian Jewish communist? Why is he so left-wing when he made all his money in stocks speculation and benefited profoundly from the capitalist system?

One must start with Soros' father, who hated Austria-Hungary because he was forced into the army and taken prisoner during the Great War. He escaped from Siberia to found Esperanto, the failed "international-language" magazine in Hungary. Of course, for anyone familiar with the Ugro-Finnish group of languages (Hungarian, Finnish), this move away from his mother-tongue is understandable, but it also underscores his social position, which was socialist even as he moved to England in 1947. Why? The Soros family survived Fascism unscathed and their beloved socialism was only just about to burgeon in Hungary shortly after the end of World War II...

Why did most immigrants come to the West from the East at the time? Economic circumstances. Poverty in eastern Europe was rampant and communism with its big government mealy-mouthed bureaucracy would never make it better. Why not sponge off the benevolent, hard-working capitalists...?

After George Soros graduated from LSE (having exhausted his Quaker support and used up his female-tutor "relationship"), he spent several years as a travelling salesman, Willy Lowman style, which were the "worst times of his life," as he said, roaming around, begging for anyone to employ him. Finally, he did find a cozy post trading the newly created Coal and Steel Community shares (SCS subsequently turned into the Common Market and became EU as we know it today).

I am well acquainted with how the Community works and my perception is that no matter how hard you try to "implement" democracy into big government, it never works. There is an endless number of doors, departments, stages in the decision-making hierarchy. Even the best-minded people are literally stuck in their place like a cog in a slow-moving chain waiting its turn on the wheel. The wheel gets larger and larger, moving slower and slower – until it moves so invisibly slowly that nothing gets ever done. I have never been so well paid for doing so little as when I had my own office next to the Minister of DG1a in Brussels – I have also never been as frustrated and never felt as helpless since...

Apparently, this system was something Soros knew only too well how to use to his benefit. Unlike the always busy capitalist bees, contemplative communists will always study the system in order to learn how to use it to their personal benefit. Soros' economic "philosophy" is founded on Karl Popper who based his economic theory on Marx: ideas influence market... Need I say more?

Ten years after roaming England as a door-to-door salesman-pauper, Soros founded his first offshore investment fund, shortly after his first hedge fund, based in Curacao, Dutch Antilles, where he invested $4mil of other peoples' money and, since 1973, profited 20% annually. We have all seen enough NBC Scammers, Suckers, and Scoundrels to realize that 20% annual profit is a Madeoff profit based on skimming off other peoples' money...

All in all, in the last 50 years, Soros has not made a cent doing honest work. He thus serves as a good example, true paragon, to all communist and socialist youth.

Democratic Socialism - 21st Century Socialism
or
How a Bus Driver Can Steer a Country

Venezuela's capital Caracas, today: soldiers in black helmets, military fatigues and bulletproof jackets; a fleet of 400 police-soldier motorcycles sweeps through narrow, crumbling, streets followed by trucks with armed SWAT-like teams; helicopters hover above shining light on the poor dilapidated dwellings. Eyes full of fear peer through chinks in walls. Street checkpoints were set up. Snipers and men in fatigues move above from roof to roof as if they were strolling through a local park. Officers with heavy weaponry are scouring alleys looking for...

Allegedly, two criminals were on the run. Locals know better though. After years of socialist parades, intimidation, starvation into submission, terrors of modern democratic socialism under Maduro, they know that this OLP "exercise" is there to intimidate the common Venezuelan who might, after all, have another "coup" in mind.

The Operation Liberation and Protection, or OLP, began in July 2015. It is the country's 23rd anti-crime initiative since President Hugo Chávez took office and launched his Bolivarian revolution in 1999. It is the third since his protegé, Maduro, began his term after Chávez died in 2013. Meanwhile, crime is on the rise, because people have nothing to eat, and – after the raids like the one described above which took place last week and during which over 120 homes belonging to common, mostly poor, Venezuelan people were razed to the ground – they have nowhere to live.

Being sick in Venezuela today is practically a death sentence. Blackouts last for weeks. People have nothing to eat or drink and very limited access to information. Drinking water is rationed and things like bread and toilet paper are available only on the black market. Basic care to people cannot be provided – not even in hospitals, because even basic instruments need electricity to function. However, if you openly defy Maduro and speak against the "regime," your house will be raided, razed to the ground and you will be taken away never to be seen or heard from again.

If this sounds like Orwell to you or some science fiction more cruel than the Handmaid's Tale, you are on the right track – only – it is reality. I experienced this reality myself when I visited Romania in 1987 when Ceausescu was in power. Will people ever learn…?

I am asking this question, because they had a choice. Nicolás Maduro has been the President of Venezuela since 14 April 2013, after winning the second presidential election after Chávez's death, with 50.61% of the votes against the opposition's candidate Henrique Capriles Radonski who had 49.12% of the votes. Prejudice and indoctrination won the elections. Perhaps, perhaps not – we will never know because the election was contested and the Supreme Court with all justices substituted by Maduro decreed in his favor.

Coincidentally, Radonski is a smart, educated, pro-capitalist entrepreneur who helped launched Kraft Foods in Venezuela and kept inviting western investment and enterprise. Unfortunately, he happens to be white and Jewish. Maduro won the elections with this motto: "Zionism, along with capitalism, are responsible for 90% of world poverty and imperialist wars." [literal quote from Maduro's campaign] "It is the evil imperialist, the fat cat capitalist that exploits the people and causes all our shortages!" yells Maduro from his opulent palace and goes to China for another $50bil money-for-oil loan. He is not starving – he is living in the lap of luxury! – and as long as other socialist "democrats" are supporting him, he will stay in power. Hamas and Palestine declared support for Maduro, as did Iranian supreme leader Khamenei.

What has our President Barack Hussein Obama done? Last year, he declared Venezuela a "National Security Threat," which is another "red line in the sand," soon to be erased by the winds of common ideology. This year, after Maduro usurped total power, suspended the Constitution by declaring a "State of Emergency" and continues acting by decree (fiat) without approval of Assembly (Venezuelan one-house Congress) with complete power of Venezuelan police and military in his grasp, our President lectures our youth about "bathroom policies" and Trump's language and his girlfriends!

Finally, what Senator Sanders is proposing here is exactly from Maduro-Chavez playbook. Chavez was a full-blown Marxist, especially after the infamous coup against him in 2002, when his grasp on power tightened and his Marxist ideology took a new lease on life. In a 2009 speech to the national assembly, he said: "I am a Marxist to the same degree as the followers of the ideas of Jesus Christ (are Christians) and the liberator of America, Simon Bolivar (are Venezuelan)." No doubt, he was a Marxist to the same extent to which Maduro and Sanders are, but mixing in Simon Bolivar...? Bolivar was an educated pro-capitalist Enlightenment entrepreneur. Maduro is a bus drive without a high school diploma. What is even more appalling, Jesus Christ was not a power-hungry socialist spitting evil and executing those who disagreed with him!

Today, Venezuela follows what Chavez started. Among the initiated, it is referred to as "revisionist Marxism" and publicly touted as "democratic socialism." Various attempts at overthrowing Chavez had only served to further radicalize him. In January 2005, he began openly proclaiming the ideology of "Socialism of the 21st Century."

Socialism of the 21st Century is Marxist Revisionism, also known as "proletarian reformism," familiar to us as "democratic socialism." This is not "capitalism tempered by socialist compassion" (as Sanders and Clinton would have you believe), but socialism, which has realized it cannot exist without capitalism: China sponges on US, Venezuela leeches on China... "Don't look the gift horse in the mouth, but whip him blind if he don't move!" Excuse my French, but "president" Maduro is a bus driver without a high-school diploma. We need to use the language everyone will understand.

In conclusion, modern "Democratic Socialists" can either educate themselves, read Hayek, Orwell, Rand,… or they can go to Venezuela and try it out.

The English Language
and the Totality of Tolerance

According to a recently conducted public survey, over 20% of American households do not speak English at home. The other day, I had a Verizon technician over and he asked me about my accent – so I asked him about his. Although he was born in this country (both his parents were "illegal immigrants," he proudly told me) he did not learn to speak English until the age of 6 when he went to school. At home, they still speak Spanish, even today.

20% is staggering but it might be even more. Why? Is it because people are naturally lazy and prefer the easiest way to communicate? Is it because the young want to be respectful of the old? Language carries with it cultural ties and background which the old generation may not want the youth to forget...

I began to learn English deep in the communist block where English was a prohibited "capitalist language." There were no textbooks, radio, television in English. There was no internet... My father gave me a four volume book from World War II he himself had used to learn English. Sometimes, I would walk outside with earplugs in my ears, trying to eliminate the language I did not want to speak: the language of the communists. I admired and craved everything American. An empty bottle of CocaCola I found on a beach in Yugoslavia was the Symbol of Life, Liberty and Happiness to me!

I certainly know what it feels like to live in a non-English speaking environment trying to learn the language you love. It is incomprehensible to me that people anywhere could have such a lukewarm attitude to the language of the country which has adopted them and provided them and their families with a new home – and what a home it is!

Are they indifferent on purpose? Indifference to the language implies indifference to the culture which the language represents. Ultimately, if they do not speak the language and do not even bother to try to learn and perfect their knowledge, it shows indifference to the country they live in.

Language is an indelible part of our Being. Being without language is impossible. Language makes us grow, love, conquer, overcome, reconcile and die in peace. We even dream in a certain language. At an attorneys' meeting, I was recently asked if I dreamt in English. You know what? Even if I did not, I would never ever admit it. What do you think, I looked at the man, I am as American as you (I thought) perhaps even more, because I had to fight for it, struggle, achieve it and deserve it – and I know what it feels like not to be one. To me, it felt like not even being human...

The New Left Universal Grammarian Noam Chomsky would reply that language is an abstraction and that English is not any better or any worse than some other language. No wonder Chomsky is one of the pillars of political correctness and the "totality of tolerance" it imposes upon us... What would my response be?

First, I do not use an "abstraction" to make my mark on the world! The more concrete the language I use, the better our communication will be. If my students ask me what I meant, I have to repeat what I said in a more concrete fashion, which is more understandable. It is not the fault of the people that they do not understand what the President allegedly means, purports or intends...

The approach of the left is different: the more smudged the meaning, the better – because it can contain all the "minorities." To "wipe it clean – like with a cloth" is what they do with our language! Yet, for all the enclosure and enveloping generosity, such a language is being eviscerated of the culture it represents – to the point that, much like its proponents, it will soon contain all-and-nothing in one. I grew up in Doublespeak myself, so I know the process – and the consequences.

Second, the English language is better because it represents the most advanced nations in the world: the United States of America, Great Britain, Canada, Australia and a host of others where our culture and faith took root. It is the most genial language with a rigid grammatical structure, which is absolutely logical and easy to grasp. We do not have three verbs to be, like the Spanish do, our verb has a logical position in the sentence – subject-verb-object-adverbial – unlike, for instance, German (where one needs to read till the very end to ascertain the meaning, as the verb is the last word in the sentence), and I'd rather not go into comparisons to such messy languages as Arabic or Chinese. Why on Earth would our students be encouraged to study Chinese?! It is a complete waste of time! It will take a Chinese person of average intelligence one tenth of the time to learn basic English. Moreover, time spent learning a language is very much wasted if we are not going to use it.

Finally, our language is not only a measure of our national identity, but it is also a part of our inner selves. It is virtually impossible to forget or "get rid of" the language we were taught as children. People often ask if the Syrian refugees or other immigrants want to assimilate. From my personal experience: it takes not just 100% of the will, but also inner desire for the new country and its culture, self-identity with the people and rejection of everything old. That is very hard to achieve and takes many years.

I am not afraid for English though. English is the richest, most widespread language in the world and English-teaching profession is a trillion dollar industry on which even many non-native English speakers thrive. No other language has the same ability assimilate foreign terms and expressions, to "anglicize" them and assimilate. This also suggests to me that no other country has the ability to assimilate as many cultures and foreign nationals than the largest English-speaking country in the world, the United States of America – provided that they want to be assimilated and that we insist on their assimilation.

Why would you not want to speak English at home? If I lived in Mexico, I would definitely want to learn as much as I could about the culture, language and people. I would not sit at home like a pumpkin but go out, sign up for extra evening classes, pay a private tutor (if I could) to come to my home. Hearing the news about people not speaking English at home, I wonder whether there is not some internal resistance to English in them because of the culture it represents – our, American culture?! English is being relegated to some technical function, communicative need of the lowest common denominator. These new immigrants will never learn the beauty of our language and culture if they do not read Huck Finn and Henry James, if they are taught to despise our Founding Fathers, and instead of Shakespeare, Milton, Pope and Dryden study asinine feminist poetry and post-modern multicultural babble and blather.

Instead of learning English and absorbing our culture, people watch the news in Vietnamese, Chinese, Korean, Spanish... They speak with accents and demand translators at official meetings, in court, at depositions, etc. This costs money and time. I have lately had trouble understanding people on the phone – the accents are so poor they literally show lack of regard for the English language and our culture. They simply learn the absolute minimum necessary to get a job – and sometimes not even that! The English language is becoming shorn of the culture it represents. The fear that many Americans express by the Tea Party Motto "Take our country back!" is fully justifiable, caused by the lack of respect for our culture and our system of government. It is thus a rational fear, which can never be called "prejudice."

20% means that approximately 70 million people (who call themselves Americans!) do not speak English at home, which means they live in a different cultural environment, indifferent to our culture, language, history and values. They are "AINOs" – Americans in Name Only – and, probably, not even that if many of them treasure their original names (e.g. Jorge Ramos, various Muhammads Salamis etc.). Why would I want to be called something like "Chlebnickova" and correct people each time they pronounce it?! Everyone is given the option to "Americanize" their name at the Naturalization ceremony. I suppose that in itself should weed the chaff from the grain.

So our country is divided by this linguistic and cultural totality of tolerance into completely separate, not very tolerant segments that care little for whether we stand united as long as they can stand on their cultural roots and no-one touches their property. Yes, they are also "SINOs" Socialists in Name Only, because: "What I have is none of your business, what you have belongs to me and let's spread your wealth!" There were many "mottoes" and sayings like these where I was growing up. You see, Doublespeak is Doublethink is Doubledo. Example: Mrs. Clinton. It is not lying exactly what she does – it is Doublethink: when I "think for you" it's different from when I think for/of myself.

As you must be rather depressed by now, let me conclude by saying that America stands on extremely strong roots: our republican system of government with its checks and balances is the best in the world and will not give in – provided that the quality of our core does not diminish and we do not let the totality of tolerance take away our Constitution and our Bill of Rights. Ultimately, the quality of the nation boils down to the quality of the individual. As our language is what makes or breaks us, we must insist on everyone speaking proper, polite English. Being polite and being politically correct is not the same thing, as we all know. Let's not get schlonged by schlemiels who would like to see our hands and feet tied by our tongues. We are a Judeo-Christian nation with strong Protestant ethics. If you don't like it, go back to where they speak YOUR language!

Foreign Policy

The only purpose of foreign policy is to further national security and commercial geopolitical interests of the nation conducting the policy. The best foreign policy leads to maximum benefit for the nation and its growing impact on other nations. Foreign policy is self-destructive – unless it is selfish, materialistic, Machiavellian, realpolitik oriented on clear-cut national goals.

B.H. Obama is a quasi-communist ideologue whose sole aim is to bring nations together in a Wilsonian New World Order where the whole world will sit at a round table and peacefully discuss one another's problems trying to help each other and maximize the other party's benefits while not diminishing one's own. We call that a "policy of appeasement" or "leading from behind."

Both of these terms are antithetical: a policy of appeasement is not a policy but a tactical step which has a place in a larger strategy, which we do not have. Why? Obama lacks wisdom. Wisdom is judgment in action, which only great, experienced generals can provide. Obama never listens to his generals, changes them like socks, demotes, fires the good ones, and keeps the kowtowing aye-sayers. What is more a policy of "appeasement" implies you "appease" someone who is offending you, i.e. is at war with you. However, if you do not recognize this fact for what it is, then a "policy of appeasement" means just looking the other way – no more, no less. It leaves you fumbling for words, like Kerry did during his "deconfliction" meeting with Russian foreign minister Lavrov.

Next, "leading from behind" is what high-ranking generals afraid of combat or unable to fight used to do in the past. Granted, it is possible to "lead from behind," but the general must have sufficient information and be constantly in action, engaged – otherwise "leading from behind" means "leading behind," leading back, retreating from action, letting the enemy take over.

Our Commander-in-Chief is not only disengaged, playing golf or sleeping (during Benghazi) but does not show sufficient acumen, skill and situational awareness in order to make a sound decision. It seems to me that every blogger on the internet in more patriotic and knows more about foreign policy than President Obama, who is completely withdrawn, uninterested in our national standing, our benefits and prosperity. Yet, we have so many bright, smart, experienced men – all of them brave and many of them wise... For sure, all braver and wiser than Mr. Golfer-in-Chief.

"Either you are with us or you are with the terrorists," said president Bush on 9/11 2001. In political science, this is referred to as a "hegemony of powers" or "binary" understanding of the world. We have lived through it during the Cold War years where you were either with Soviet Union or against them, and vice versa. It is applicable in moments of crisis, impending war, when there is a threat to national insecurity. Its reintroduction by President Bush was purposefully intended to minimize the influence of Russia in the Middle East while sharpen the focus of our foreign policy and thus strengthen our geopolitical scope and standing.

When we left, as we all know, Iraq was stabilized, and the apparent need for the binary understanding of the world disappeared. I state "apparent" because Russia was watching, as was Iran. Anyone who read Hobbes' Leviathan knows that it is impossible to introduce an "Obama-order" based on absolute equality and idealistic pacifistic negotiations in good will for the other party. This epitomizes communist thinking. All nations, just as all people, have foibles and will behave selfishly whenever they can. It is not wrong, it is human.

What Obama has been unsuccessfully attempting during his two terms in the Office is similar to what President Wilson conceived of (also unsuccessfully) with his League of Nations at the end of World War I. We should note the similarities: both Obama and Wilson have been progressives theoreticians and although Wilson was much better educated, they shared equally skewed understanding of statehood and foreign policy. They also both received the Nobel Peace Prize and wanted to be admired and remembered as, in Woodrow Wilson's words, "savior of the world!"

Whence this fundamental lack of understanding of how the world works? It is my suspicion that neither Wilson nor Obama ever fully comprehended the concept of statehood. This modern concept dates back to the Peace of Westphalia in 1648, which ended the Thirty Years' War: European states agreed to respect one another's sovereignty and territorial integrity. One of the parties to the Treaty was Holy Roman Empire, which consisted of many nationalities. These soon realized that the concept of statehood meant the right to self-determination, laws in their own language, borders and currency. What we call "Balkanization" started long before the Great War...

Significantly, Hobbes' Leviathan was published in 1651, following the Peace of Westphalia, and those who read it would have foreseen that there is always diversity in unity – but not vice versa! Chiefly, states always crave for independence and always compete with one another. Even the peace negotiations treated states as if they were self-interested multi-national corporations. Needless to say that this realistic approach worked well for 150 years, until Napoleon came trying to take over the Holy Roman Empire and with it all of Europe.

Subsequent to Napoleon, the "Concert of Europe" was established in Vienna, whereupon it was determined that any inter-state aggression by one party would be counterbalanced by a "concert" of powers mitigating such aggression. The Balance of Powers system arose: Prussia, Austria, and Russia formed Holy Alliance, a conservative "federation" based on Christianity and traditional monarchy. Britain joined a few weeks later. However, this Alliance lasted only briefly, as the revolutions of 1848, rise of Marxism and nationalism shook Europe and prevented a lasting peace.

At the onset of the 19th century, the Balance of Powers emerged as the scales of Triple Alliance (Germany, Austria-Hungary, Italy) versus the Entente Powers (England and Ireland, France, Russia). Naturally, geopolitical view was different from the Isle of "splendid insulation" – Britain has never really ceased to view the rest of Europe as a board of checkers where powers align in their own interests. It was not until Germany invaded Belgium (which had been a neutral entity for over a hundred years, since the Peace of Vienna in 1814) that England entered the Great War scuffle.

Interestingly, by the end of this war, Wilson would still have been viewed more as a cook than a prophet. Who would have ever thought that Europe could diverge from the Peace of Westphalia and their precious balance of powers? After World War II, situation changed. Cooperation was needed to rebuild what had been destroyed. The founding of the United Nations in 1945 was an idealistic spur, hope for a lasting peace based on a New World Order. In 1951 in Paris, Under American influence, European states started to diverge from the Balance of Powers and the Peace of Westphalia. The first step was the creation of European Coal and Steel Community (ECSC) under the new heading of "supranationalism." Subsequent establishment of EEC and its transition into EC and EU has been a long process of tearing away from the Westphalian system of statehood and sovereignty.

However, even before the influx of refugees and today's crisis (which clearly shows lack of cooperation and competency in dealing with "supranational security"), EU was looked upon with distrust. No wonder, with their secret behind-closed-doors proceeding of the European Council and Council of Ministers, they brought less democracy and decision-making power to the people. By the same token, peoples – which is to say: nations – do not say "I am EU" but "I am English, French, German..." The national identity has not been erased by this supra-national monster.

To be fair, UN has been successful in one respect – we have prevented World War III and nuclear war. Knock on wood. However, it cannot "govern" as a supreme body overseeing a supranational entity consisting of the whole world. What we see in Europe as well as in the United States is longing for statehood and identity. It is that identity which had arisen from the Peace of Westphalia and given rise to independently competing nations. After all, we are only human and we want "to belong" to a nation, be a part of some clearly identified whole, not a potlach of cultures, an amalgam of races where no-one really knows who they are. I wonder, Mr. President Obama who do you cheer for as a "citizen of the world?" World peace? If so, you remind me of the innocent looking beauty queen pageant answering a well-rehearsed question: world peace and love everyone. Certainly. Have you ever thought about the fact that when you love everyone you love no-one? That is an old communist dilemma. I will let you sleep on it.

Thus, President Obama acts as if this world-wide supranational government existed as his creation, a matter-of-fact, as if he presided as a benevolent king over the imaginary "Concert of All Nations" who shall follow the wishes of His Royal Obamaness. First, his Iran Treaty is a "giveaway," not a deal. For a deal, there must be give-and-take on both parts. Second, his approach to our immigration and national security shows that he is incapable of conceiving of statehood as nationhood – to him, statehood does not exist and nationhood has only one meaning: a part of the United Nations, which is yet another "giveaway," for are we not financing majority of UN resolutions, actions, humanitarian and other support – without receiving anything of value in return? Next, like Chamberlain, he travels abroad as an apologetic messenger of peace, and war breaks out the moment he leaves. If you trust him, you shall be sorely disappointed – unless you are his golfing buddy.

Meanwhile, Iran is engaging in the bait-and-bleed strategy, letting US and Russia engage while watching and waiting. Kerry continues useless trips to Vienna and London (Jan. 13-15), meeting with Saudi Arabia's Foreign Minister Adel al-Jubeir. Saudis have cut ties with Iran, responding to the storming of its embassy in Tehran over Riyadh's execution of a Shi'ite Muslim cleric. Saudis are in a similar situation we had been in in Lybia. As a result of Obama's misunderstanding of what is going on, we have witnessed the birth of a new IRAN-IRAQ-RUSSIA (Shi'ite) coalition of "progressive" Muslims who want to kill us. Last week, Iran's

Supreme Leader Ayatollah Ali Khamenei was seen on Iran's state television threatening that "divine vengeance will befall Saudi politicians!"

Saudi Arabia represents a conservative Sunni monarchy. Thus, the divide between Suni and Shi'ite coalitions parallels our internal Democrat-Republican schism, which is probably why Obama sides with Shi'ites, although it threatens our very existence. Paradoxically, we are back to 9/11 and to President Bush's statement: "You are either with us or against us." Binary understanding is the modern Balance of Powers understanding. However, Obama wants to conciliate parties instead of building useful coalitions. The only way to prevent further turmoil is to establish permanent military bases in all countries around the world, renew the missile defense program in Poland and the Czech Republic, stay away from European Union's internal politics, and build our national defense at home: borders, armies, militias. Empower citizens of the United States and weed out our enemies.

My foreign policy in the Middle East is as follows: support the Suni coalition so that Suni-Shi'ite powers are in balance. Otherwise, do not interfere. Further, definitely equip the Kurds, let them have a separate state if they can handle it; and, of course, give Israel everything they need to defend their nationhood (superior nuclear defense capability and fleet backing). We need to focus on building our civilization. We are a nation of builders. But the whole world must know that if someone steps in our way with malicious intent, they shall be destroyed. As General Patton said, take no prisoners. If there are any left, send them to hard labor – build for US! You know what that means, Mr. Obama – make Guantanamo a naval base with a missile defense system. ISIS is history. Iran will be too if they don't stop calling us the Big Satan.

Clash of Civilizations

Several politicians, as well as media, have recently referred to the conflict between East and West as a "clash of civilizations." Every westerner of average intellect and historical awareness knows about the Persian expansion from Marathon and Thermopylae to the siege of Vienna two thousand years later. Nonetheless, some notable academicians and students of the "liberal arts" shy from this term as either obsolete, overcome, or inappropriate. Their solution lies in a "social funnel" of absolute tolerance in the system of democratic socialism.

Had President Obama been correct in his assessment of ISIS as "JV team," the term "clash of civilizations" would be inappropriate. After all, what kind of "civilization" does a bunch of hooligan mass murderers and suicide bombers represent? However, he meant this as a comparison to Al-Qaida, not as an absolute measure of the degree of evil. All terrorist organizations that currently threaten us are united under the banner of Islam, which makes them part of Islamic world, culture, civilization. They are ultimately destructive of the civilization which gave them birth, as I elucidate below.

President Obama's statement is supported by the liberal rationale that we can absorb that which aims to destroy us, because "there is room for everybody." Well, there is not. The world is growing smaller in proportion to the growth of global population. Evil, much like anti-matter, is omnipresent and hard to see – until it strikes us.

Liberalism also stands on the shaky, feeble feet of self-deceiving viewpoint that Europe is the most advanced of cultures because it has successfully assimilated all cultures, habits, traditions, religions, languages and peoples. This is clearly false. Not only is there an internal struggle and constant splintering (so-called "Balkanization") present on different levels across the EU, but European communities are as little tolerant and capable of assimilation as Harlem is of white collar Wall Street "wasps." There are still nations that are 99% Caucasian (e.g. Poland, Czech

Republic, Slovakia...) and even those that are endeavoring to be "politically correct" will not assimilate someone who is simply the "odd one out" (Sweden, Norway, Denmark, rural Austria and Germany).

Another error of judgment (and knowledge) must be attributed to the New Left and their socialist followers: the political organization across EU is not that of "democratic socialism" but either a multi-party social democracy or parliamentarian system and hereditary monarchy – or all of the three combined. Linguistic differences project cultural differences and contribute to the lack of overall cohesion, which is forced upon Europeans by politicians as a market and survival necessity. Europe is thus moving from a free market economy ever more to a planned, centralized system, which most Europeans abhor and detest.

It follows that Europe is not a cultural entity: Italian cities are different from village areas, north of Italy completely different from the south, both are different from French cities and villages, and the differences between those and British "splendid insulation" cannot be overemphasized. How can it be a political entity if it is not a cultural one? Spliced, stapled, and Band-aided together, European states keep professing their independence and not a year passes by without some referendum somewhere about independence (England, Greece, Czech Republic...).

European history is that of constant struggle and political machinations among the "powers" in order to preserve a "balance." Nations have always proudly asserted their independence by borders, language, political system, currency... With the rise of EU, all these fall like a deck of cards. What remains? What remains indeed if we cannot call Europe one "culture?" It is arguable whether we can call it one "civilization." Does such a reference even make sense in the context of the constant flow of information, assimilation of terms, language and custom exchange etc.?

Yet, in the United States, we seem to look up to Europe as if it were in possession of some political balm on the modern ailments of cultural and racial divisiveness. Of course, we are blithely unawares that Europe is looking up to us, trying to copy our solutions. After all, "United States of Europe" was something Napoleon had dreamt up when he saw how our forefathers dealt with the British – by unity and resolve. In unity lies strength; division precedes fall!

We had had our fundamental struggle (the Civil War) five or six generations ago. However, that fight was not "civilizational" – not in the way the Greeks had fought the Persians or the Habsburgs tried to resist and curb the Ottoman expansion in the sixteenth and seventeenth century. Had the South won, our existence would not have been fundamentally different. Slavery would have been abolished later, under economic and evolutionary pressure, and all would be well again – because we belong to the same civilization.

What defines a civilization? Religion. Currently, we have the following major civilizations: Western, Slavic-Orthodox, Confucian, Buddhist, Hindu, Islamic, and a developing African civilization. If Catholicism prevails in Africa, the whole continent will join western democracies and develop accordingly; if Islam prevails, Africa will continue as a mishmash of totalitarian regimes (unless Islam undergoes a reform and separates the Church from the State).

Naturally, all states and nations we conceive of as one "civilization" also have similar customs, habits, mythology – and belong to akin language families. It is only natural that French, Spanish, and Italian are similar (Romanesque, Latin cognates) as well as that German, Dutch, Swedish, Norwegian and intersecting dialects are similar. The Fins and Hungarians are odd ducks out. There will always be some. In order to belong to the same civilization, small nations must be culturally subjected to the large ones, e.g. Czech Republic and Austria to Germany, Portugal to Spain, Ireland to England, Finland to Norway and Sweden. What choice do they have? We have seen that in World War II.

English has assimilated every language it encountered during its existence: Romanesque, Germanic, even Arabic to a small degree. Thus, English has become the most successful modern language, substituting Latin in science and French in diplomacy. No wonder we feel so personal about political correctness and people who are unwilling to learn English, presenting us with incorrigible, incomprehensible foreign accents. It is not their accents that bother us – it is their invasion of our culture and the fact that we are being forced into submission. English language does not merely represent a state or a nation, and it is not merely a means of communication. English language is a way of life! It represents our culture, our personal identity!

Customs, traditions, legends, myths, superstitions, even language usage (idioms, proverbs etc.) are all related to the religion of the particular civilization. We cannot limit our focus here to one state or nation. Have you ever wondered how come immigrants from western Europe find it easy to assimilate and become American? We have the same roots, of course. The further east you go, the more difficult it will be for the immigrants to assimilate.

There exist exceptions, but these were created by history and evolution. For instance, many Russians have French and German roots and are much more "westernized" than their orthodox counterparts or even some nation-states which had purposefully and with great verve separated themselves from "Mother Russia" after the fall of communism. For instance, the people of Ukraine feel more "European" than Russian because of their geographic and historical position. They are comparable to Poland in that Ukraine also functioned as a "buffer zone" between Russia and western Europe in the past. Western Ukraine also used to be part of Czechoslovakia…

Whenever assimilation becomes forced "from above" and thus destructive of the religion (habits and customs, eventually also language) of the community, it will be resisted, because the community is in fear for its very survival. Rightfully so. It is the same with every individual: when you take my privacy, my beliefs, my freedoms – I am going to fight back! When you take the community's religion, its distinct identity, its constitution – the community will fight back! Borders are only lines in the sand compared to the borders that define us as belonging to the Judeo-Christian tradition.

In evolutionary terms, phylogeny mimics ontogeny: the development of the species corresponds to that of the individual and vice versa. Civilizations and nations are born, grow up, develop, reach retirement and fall apart just like each individual member of the given civilization does. While our nation, the United States of America, is still a young, beautiful girl, she is much older and stronger than she looks, because she is part of the Western Civilization.

We feel very personal about our customs, religion, and language because they define us and make us who we are. "Make America Great again" and "Take our Country Back" are mottoes which represent how we feel as members of our civilization, the civilization which is under assault. Anyone who invades our privacy and wants to take away our religion, our guns, mutilates our language and rapes our Lady Justice is our enemy! The enemy cannot be "assimilated." The enemy must be destroyed in order for our civilization to survive.

Interventionism and Isolationism
in Our Foreign Policy

President Obama's supranationalism is not anything new in our foreign policy. What is new is his being supranationalist on the one hand and isolationist on the other. He has often defined himself as a man absolved of ideology, a pragmatist who will do whatever is necessary under the circumstances. Necessary for what? Necessary to achieve a certain goal, which, in his case, has been purely ideological. What is more, he is discordant and ambivalent to the very core. War calls for intervention: you must win the war first, then negotiate the peace. What is more, you cannot change venue. Very rarely can you choose the terrain. Has Obama ever read Sun Tzu? I do not think so. Has he read Alinsky and Mao and heard of Che? I am certain he has.

It was with President Wilson that our move to internationalism and interventionism began. Quite frankly, it was also a product of Theodore Roosevelt's and William Howard Taft's pressure, although both had fundamental disagreements with Wilson. First, Roosevelt despised Wilson as a "college president with an astute and shifty mind, a hypocritical ability to deceive plain people." His policy was "utter folly... a milk-and-water righteousness unbacked by force." Even before Lusitania, neither Roosevelt nor Taft could see any lasting peace with Germany, or even neutrality, as a wise option. Wilson, on the other hand, viewed the British policy of "starving Germans into submission" as inhumane.

You may have noticed the terms "utter folly" and "inhumane." How does "utter folly" differ from Trump's "our leadership is stupid?" The left calls us "inhumane" when we want to apply breaks on immigration. As of today, Germany is considering moving 80,000 "migrants" away, "back," because over 600 women have come up with rape and sexual assault allegations against Muslims. Back where? Most of them want to go further "north" because they think they will get more money, better food and housing – paid for by the taxpayer. Now, vis-à-vis this dire situation, should our foreign policy experts call for isolationism or interventionism? Should they practice the policy of holier-than-thou neutrality instead?

We have always been a country of individuals, mavericks, original men of substance. In his farewell address, George Washington warned us against "entangling alliances." This advice was a two-edged sword: we did not have the power to fight another war, and – we had nothing to gain by doing so. Washington left us with a lasting legacy: if you do not have the power to conquer and if you have nothing to gain, stay out of it.

Why should we intervene in Europe's refugee problem? Can we solve it? Can we gain anything by doing so? As to ISIS, can we conquer them? Then the sober pragmatist (that Obama is holding himself out to be) should say: Go ahead and do it! Then, and only then, could we negotiate from the position of power. What would George Washington do? He would stay away from EU and show the world what we mean when we draw a "red line."

The problem with both isolationism and interventionism is that they are "-isms" – that they want to see the world black-and-white. However, the world revolves in many shades, the hues of a rainbow. There is no clear-cut line separating isolationism from interventionism. In 1823, President Monroe declared a new "hands-off Europe" policy, which was isolationist toward Europe and interventionist with respect to South and Latin America. It was a good strategy, as we had won our Second War of Independence and gathered enough strength to be concerned with our national growth – industry and continental expansion. This led to predominance of isolationism, especially with rising inner tensions and ripening Civil War. A weak nation cannot fight abroad. A nation weakened by disunity cannot fight – period.

The marker of transition from what we might view as "pure isolationism" was the rising power of industry and our reaching the western frontier: in 1890, a public census declared there was no longer a "contiguous frontier" (unknown wilderness) and therefore the frontier was "closed." The impact of this realization was foreshadowed in a famous essay by Frederick Jackson Turner presented to a special meeting of the American Historical Association at the World's Columbian Exposition in Chicago, Illinois, in 1893. Apart from a certain apprehension of national "claustrophobia," Turner argued that our national drive, core, competitive self and sense of growth might be severely hampered and constricted by this sudden "closure."

It is not by coincidence that many Americans began to travel abroad at this time, mainly to Europe. To name a few: Theodore Roosevelt climbed on the top of Mont Blanc and was appointed to the Royal Society of London, Henry James visited Paris after introducing a new character to the world: the brash, bold American lady who travels to Europe on her own to face the stern aristocracy and defy local "mores" (Daisy Miller, The Portrait of a Lady), and Mark Twain carried this to new heights with his time traveler in Connecticut Yankee (of course, having already ridiculed the Americans eager to learn from scattered old stones of Italy in his Innocents Abroad)...

The first purely interventionist action came at the turn of the century: the Spanish-American War, in which we won Guantanamo. McKinley (and his "Rough Rider" Ted) was also interested in Panama and Nicaragua as well as other maritime "resorts" of strategic importance (Puerto Rico, Guam, Philippines). Roosevelt's chief influence, Alfred Thayer Mahan, was born in West Point to a professor of Naval History, man who taught Grant, Lee and other great generals of the Civil War... American Pragmatism arose from the soil and is inextricably tied to the realism of power. C.S. Peirce, Chauncey Wright, William James, John Dewey, George Herbert Mead followed in the steps of George Washington, who started as a licensed surveyor in the Shenandoah and grew into the ultimate pragmatist.

True American Pragmatism has nothing to do with "hope and change" or pursuit of harmony among nations. Indeed, if President Obama, as a man with merely legal background, is unaware of the impact of the Metaphysical Club, he cannot call himself a pragmatist. In fact, the goals of his policies appear to be anti-pragmatic in that the consequences of his actions decry and contradict the requirements of reality – because they are based on beliefs, not on facts. Therefore, no matter what President Obama does, he will always wind up in a state of incomplete, incongruous, ambivalent chaos. Unity (speaking of a nation or in military terms) cannot be based on idealism, but only on reality. Divisiveness results from substituting ideas for reality, creating symbols for abstractions, making words mean more than actions.

Idealism leads to absolutism because no corrective measures in reality will impact abstractions in the ideal world. No doubt Mahan and Roosevelt hated Wilson-Bryan administration of righteousness and appeasement because of this "academic idealism" of "nation-building" and persistent shying from war at all costs. Every -ism puts blindfolds on Common Sense and points him in the direction of another -ism. Battling Isms breed nothing but contempt in a sane, rational onlooker. Pancho Villa called Woodrow Wilson an "evangelizing professor..." Theodore Roosevelt had probably more respect for Villa than for Wilson. To paraphrase Roosevelt: You cannot have peace without victory and you cannot be too proud to fight! For someone to win, someone else must lose – that is the true teaching of pragmatism.

A decade of Jezz Age, the Roaring Twenties, flapper and art deco followed World War I. This was marked by business growth, lower taxes, tariffs (under Harding) and support of all private enterprise. As President Coolidge famously said: "The Business of America is Business." It is not by coincidence that we heard this repeated after World War II by Engine Charlie (US Secretary of Defense to Eisenhower): "What is good for General Motors is good for America." Harding-Coolidge-Hoover sequence was a "swing" back to isolationism, which meant conservatism and home values. The depression years also required special

90

economic measures which did not give much room or leeway to any deep concern with what was going on abroad.

However, regardless of the economic situation at home, it would have been impossible to stay completely neutral in World War II – just as it had been in World War I. Wilson may have won his second term on the banner of the jingle that "he kept us out of war" (similar policy contributed to F.D.R.'s third re-election in 1940) but there is no such thing as "complete neutrality." Even in the tradition of "international concert of peace" and a "community of power" (Wilson's terms) there were bound to arise "entangling alliances" out of sheer necessity.

It was through the acid tests of world wars that the United States emerged as the "Arsenal of Democracy." This term had been coined at the end of the Great War, referring to Wilson's internationalism, but it did not become well known until the Land-Lease Act during F.D.R.'s administration, when the world requested help – and help we did: Great Britain, France... but also China and Russia gleaned significant aid from US. John Winthrop's "City upon a Hill" metaphor, which originally referred to us as a group of the brave chosen to be "tested" under the watchful eye of the rest of humanity, acquired a new meaning: we were a beacon to the rest of the world, a shining example worth admiration and imitation, whose purpose it was to go abroad spreading democracy.

America's charitable effort in helping other nations has since been looked down upon as both a naïve effort based on misunderstanding of local conditions, and a self-serving desire to appropriate and expand – an indirect result or repercussion of the "closing" of our frontier. No doubt, Frederick Jackson Turner had had a similar phenomenon in mind in 1893. It is contrary to our naval-military experience (Mahan) and also to what the Father of our Country had warned us against: entangling alliances. Our efforts in Iraq, Afghanistan, Libya... have been doomed to failure. The only legacy we take away is that of blame. In Europe, they say we go everywhere "for oil." In China and Russia, they see us as "land grabbing" and "greedy," no matter what we do.

We do not help other nations because it would make us stronger militarily nor do we go around the world "nation-building" with an eye on oil wells. We do it because we are good-natured people with strong Judeo-Christian values, morally stable and sturdy. What makes us strong is not what we have but who we are, how we got to be where we are. Trump speaks our minds when he says: "So what if Russia does the job for us?" We are tired of world's ingratitude for our fallen heroes, for our efforts and energy expanding in teaching others how to be better.

The Swedes gave Obama Nobel Peace Prize. They gave one to Wilson too. So we go abroad to help the world and our Commander-in-Chief gets a medal from a committee of socialist fogies totally abstracted from reality... I grew up looking up to the United States, the Land of the American Dream, thinking: it is a universal dream, alive everywhere... for it has always been the engine in my chest, spurring me on. Today, many people do not see the forest for the trees. The American Dream is a very definite pragmatic road out of serfdom, the untrodden path of a maverick who cannot be uprooted from reality.

F.D.R. found it virtually impossible to persuade the citizens of the United States, who had barely recovered from the Great Depression, to support more than covert aid and intervention – until Pearl Harbor. Just like on 9/11/2001, it took a massive attack on the mainland to mobilize the American interventionist psyche. War is always in part a matter of revenge. The other part is conquest. Trump is powerful because we know if another Bay of Pigs came, he would not blink first, and if there was another 9/11, he would not hesitate to fire the missiles of revenge at the enemy.

Since F.D.R., we went to Korea, Vietnam, Yugoslavia, Iraq, Afghanistan... all either hell-holes of nationalism or tribal primitivism. We could not understand their habits, customs, culture, we only deemed it not compliant with ours. Modern push for diversity is accompanied by the supranationalist push for "equality." What President Obama does not understand is that you cannot have your cake and eat it too: you cannot dictate supranationalism and Wilson-like world order on the one hand while staying apart, perhaps aloof, fully "non-interventionist" on the other. What is more, just like in our internal politics – when Congress is silent on a change in law requested by the President – silence speaks volumes in foreign policy. The aged motto of Von Clausewitz that "war is continuation of politics by other means" should be borne in mind when politicians cannot agree on a plan of action.

Welcome to the DEMOCRATIC United States!

Coming from the environment I hated and detested, longing for the United States with all my Soul and my Heart, I had been American before my feet ever touched the American soil. The rest was a process of waiting and overcoming all the legal hurdles. I became a citizen after 10 years of waiting and complying with the INS demands, which included mandatory return to Europe after 4 years on my HB visa, and filling in the request for a green card through the embassy in Prague. My lawyer told me that they "should comply and let me back" – thus, by leaving the United States physically, I was also running the risk that I would not be permitted to return. I was a costly hurdle, but I cleared it without major difficulties.

My language skills and knowledge of American culture served me in good stead. I had "Americanized" my name as soon as I could, after the revolution and communist fall. I was 18 then and my heart and soul was American. It was not until twelve years later that I was fortunate enough to secure a "sponsor" and arrive here. Going back after four years of my stay was not easy, as you can imagine, but I was told that there was no other way, which is true – certainly not for a white legal immigrant coming from Europe.

For four years prior to my becoming a citizen, I was not permitted to travel abroad. I could, I was told, but I would have been risking being turned down when I requested citizenship. Sometimes, prioritizing is hard. My mother was dying of cancer and died one month before I finally received my US passport. Rules are rules. We are a country of laws.

Every last Thursday of the month, 6-7000 people (and nearly twice as many family members and friends) gather at the LA Convention Center on the occasion of receiving their citizenship. It is a solemn occasion, which most of us do not take lightly. Organization is awesome and the "swearing in" moved me to tears. For all the paperwork, Kleenex was something I forgot to bring along with me.

94

I find it hard to comprehend how someone who refuses to "Americanize" their name, worships their own language and culture, refuses to speak English... can be allowed entry in a few days on a "fiancée" visa!

Another issue is the number of Korean and Hispanic families who come here legally but, as I had the occasion to witness at the swearing in, barely bother to learn a word of English, insist that people pronounce their peculiar names and write them down. Many of the people who took the Oath of Allegiance with me when I was becoming a citizen not only did not speak English – but they were permitted to take the Oath in their own language! Everything was translated and interpreted into Spanish. Finally, they played President Obama's address, which welcomed us "to the DEMOCRATIC United States!" Immediately the next ("optional") step was registration to vote. I can imagine that a person from Salvador or Venezuela does not even know that there is a Republican party and that "democratic" does not mean Democrat, or that the registration to vote is optional...

Language means much more than understanding or "getting by." Phrases, denotations, idioms and cultural ties of our childhood stay with us and, no matter how hard we try to sever them, they will return on occasion to catch us unawares, unprepared, betraying our "foreignness" in the adoptive country. This is almost akin to a foreign accent in one's thoughts... I hate it, of course, but I would fain deny it happens. I cannot imagine how it works for someone keen on the habits and culture of their birthplace. They can never ever assimilate – not to mention becoming a true American.

We all know that language means culture. Once you try to read 100 Years of Solitude in Spanish or Kant in German (you can try it with a translation in the other hand) you will understand how indelibly and inextricably the two are intertwined. There exists no exact translation or interpretation which quite corresponds to the original. Again, take it from someone who ran a translation agency and was employed by the European Community as a "language expert."

I recall how I tried to permeate the contemporary American culture by reading the Rabbit Trilogy by John Updike. I had to read it out loud to myself, record myself, play it back, learning sentences, even whole chunks of text by heart. I would look up every single word I was uncertain about, jot it down in an exercise book, finding new ways how to remember words, making up my own contexts, developing phrasal verbs and idioms with the same love some people daily weed and grow roses in their front yard.

John Updike has a special gift for capturing the common "Americanness" with all its shades of meaning and daily upheavals. What was the most difficult for me was the vocabulary tied to culture and cultural phenomena, available to everyone who lives in the United States today – brand names of kitchen products, soap operas or T.V. series... Living in a foreign land, non-English-speaking culture where, for instance, everybody uses kitchen cloths, how could one understand "paper towels" or what Kleenex means?

That is just one example of many. I also sat in a class of foreign students, all eager to learn English, all looking up to the professor (naturally the only native English speaker in the class), their eyes full of desire and what I would best call "healthy envy" saying: "I wish I could say it like that... ah!" and "What a beautiful pronunciation!" and "What is New York like?"

When he was explaining to us what "they" did on Christmas Eve and what food they ate – why, you should have seen the imagination and ravenous enquiries hurled his way! And, of course, many people abroad want to learn the "real English" with the American accent and all the power of the United States imbued in it. Who cares about: "Blimey! Have you been there indeed?" When you can say: "Yo, bro, wasn't that a blast!" You can imagine how funny it can be in a foreign language classroom when students are trying to pronounce and learn colloquial American English phrases...

This is one of the reasons that many students of English living abroad know probably more about American and British history and literature than most native speakers, for whom it is often some compulsory high school "stuff" – something to go through quickly, get the grade, and "move on." These students go to school every day, study and work hard – and dream their American Dream, abroad. Meanwhile, our students follow the ideologically biased Common Core, which teams with the prejudice of political correctness, teaching interpretations, not facts. The old saying "One original is worth a thousand interpretations," sounds more like Confucius than Obama.

One cannot learn a foreign language without learning about the culture of the country in which it is spoken. Thus, it seems to me, the right to vote in the absence of understanding the language is truly an absurdity. Section 203 of the Voting Rights Act obliges local governments to issue official translations of the ballot for minority groups. This only fosters their ignorance of our culture and our language. It also disadvantages other minorities, not strong enough to have the ballot translated. If you come from a non-Asian, non-Spanish speaking country, and you do not speak English, you will be greatly disadvantaged. How come some minorities are forced to learn English and others are not?

English is the richest, most widespread language in the world and the English-teaching profession is a trillion-dollar industry on which even many non-native English speakers thrive. No other language has the same ability assimilate foreign terms and expressions. This also suggests to me that no other country has the ability to assimilate as many cultures and foreign nationals than the largest English-speaking country in the world, the United States of America – provided that they want to be assimilated and that we insist on their assimilation!

Is assimilation not natural, something one should accept as a fact, similar to the fact that you adjust your diet to the food you can purchase in stores, no doubt different from what you were weaned on? If I lived in Mexico, I would definitely want to learn as much as I could about the culture, language and people. I would not sit at home like a pumpkin but go out, sign up for extra evening classes, pay a private tutor (if I could) to come to my home. What is more the "English-resistant" new immigrants will never learn the beauty of our culture and history – not if they do not read Huck Finn and Henry James, the "Way to Wealth" and "Poor Richard's Almanac."

It seems to me that they are actually made to "fit" our "Common Core," which despises our Founding Fathers because they were white, makes slavery something the United States created in order to discriminate, tears down the Old Glory and everything "offensive" (which includes digging up in cemeteries for great generals of the Civil War, such as Nathan Bedford Forrest – which I personally consider a crime). Add the pressure of political correctness, regulated meanings of words and the diminished ability of our own average American population to enlarge their vocabulary, improve grammar, master our history and be bold and proud of it. Watters' World and Jay Leno's "jaywalking" has shown us the abysmal gaps in knowledge of our national identity created by the Common Core and political correctness. Everybody wants to be a "citizen of the world" fighting world pollution and poverty. I realize the pathos of this vanity every time I cross the local park to the nearby pool, picking a piece of litter on the way to throw it into the trashcan a few steps away.

Seeing this mess of multiculturalism in our country – what incentive do we provide to the new immigrants to learn English and truly become proud Americans? What value do we place on citizenship? With each new "executive amnesty" and every new spending bill, the value of our citizenship decreases. To become a US citizen today means to immediately assume $200,000 of national debt per individual and to pay 40-50% taxes (property, city, state, federal... let me count the ways). Of course, people still come – because they can get "free stuff" and are still better off than in "their" countries. But why should they forsake their heritage and culture if they see ours crumbling? Who will we borrow from next – India, Iran, Russia?

You may have noticed that NBC, CNN, Aljazeera and others began to refer to the new (illegal) immigrants as "migrants." This is another PC term, which, however, means what it says: they come here temporarily to squeeze US dry and wait out the period of socialism or tyranny in their countries. They neither immigrate to the US nor emigrate out of the country of their birth – the former would imply permanent stay and the latter permanent leave. "Migrants" means our permanent resignation – absolute liberalism at work: "Come here if you want, do what you want, leave as you will, use what you can, ask what you wish!"

Such attitude creates not the Land of the Free, Home of the Brave – but another Croatia, Slovenia, Greece... a transitory country too weak to impose its laws – save, perhaps, for imposing them on law-abiding citizens who will defend and fight for the Eagle and the Statute of Liberty no matter what.

All those who come here must be as American as John Wayne and apple pie. If someone cannot learn English and know our history and political system before they ever set foot on the American soil, they are not yet ripe and fit to come here and stay. Becoming an American citizen must be the highest prize and reward they will ever achieve – as it has been for me.

Political Correctness that Matters

The term "politically correct" was coined in the case of Chisholm v. Georgia, 2 U.S. (2 Dall.) 419 (1793), where it meant not some "socially offensive" language but, rather, interpretation of laws according to the Constitution. Thus, "Constitutionally correct" and "politically correct" were synonymous. What is more, the Supreme Court in Chisholm held that once people are treated as servants to the state, not the state as a creation by the people and for the people, any conduct and speech flowing from such Constitutional distortion will become "politically incorrect."

As Justice Wilson stated: "A state, I cheerfully fully admit, is the noblest work of Man. But, Man himself, free and honest, is, I speak as to this world, the noblest work of God." [Ibid. p.463] By this he means that the state was created by Man to serve Man but Man himself was created by God. We should never forget the hierarchy of values from which we derive morals and ethical conduct. Justice Wilson then continued to cite several examples from human history, including Homer and Demosthenes, in which "politically correct" meant "classically correct," such as the appellation "the people of Athens," ergo: "the People of the United States." Politically correct thus meant legally subject to the "more perfect union" (the quote comes from the Preamble to our Constitution) which meant the Union of the United States, a confederacy, if you will, where states are treated on an equal footing, subjected to federal laws and government.

"In order therefore to form a more perfect union, to establish justice, to ensure domestic tranquility, to provide for common defense, and to secure the blessings of liberty..." – we all know these words and they ring in our ears as indelible common sense truths today. Legislative and Executive powers are vested in our Constitution. What we have seen in the last seven years, however, has been distortion upon distortion, a Three-Card Monte game of thorns played upon us by our leaders: Find the Lady –

Liberty. Where is she? He in Power provided her with "shelter."

TRANQUILITY, COMMON DEFENSE, LIBERTY – they have all been undermined and eroded by what we call "political correctness." More than that, we are losing them because we have permitted the term "politically correct" to be RADICALLY TRANSFORMED: instead of "Constitutionally correct" it means "inoffensive to anyone." If we act to preserve our borders and TRANQUILITY (domestic peace), it is not "politically correct." If we strive for COMMON DEFENSE, be it by providing our police with what they need to defend us, financing our military, managing and securing AMERICAN foreign policy and our strategy, we are not "politically correct." If we see something suspicious going on in our neighborhood but we are afraid to say something in order not to offend someone...

Alas: there lies TRUE POLITICAL CORRECNESS! When we do not stand for our Constitutional rights and liberties, then we ARE NOT POLITICALLY CORRECT in the sense in which the Supreme Court defined political correctness. To be American first, to be a patriot, to be unafraid and fight for your Constitution: that is THE ONLY POLITICAL CORRECTNESS THAT MATTERS. It is the POLITICAL CORRECTNESS OF ACTION, not that of the word.

How to Deal with Political Correctness

While we cannot cry "fire" FALSELY in a crowded theatre, thus causing panic, we can do so if there is fire. One should bear this in mind when peeking through the window at the neighbor's pipe bomb factory.

On the other hand, stating falsely anything about another's business reputation, criminal history (alleging crime), sexual disease or immoral acts constitutes libel per se. Thus, if you publicly speak about someone regarding criminal conduct they are not committing, you may be liable for libel under tort law.

However, reporting what we see as "suspicious" does not fall in this category. Rather than debating with your neighbors and family (spreading rumors may constitute slander or libel), you should call the authorities, because this may actually prevent you from being falsely accused of libel in future. Public interest outweighs an honest mistake.

There is more to the reluctance to report another than political correctness. There is more to political correctness itself, because it encompasses not merely our speech but also our conduct. Political correctness is often not even directly applied to the word itself as much as to "how" things were said, the proverbial "tone" of the speech (in Donald Trump's words). After all, people are not restrained from crossing the boundaries of decency on the internet's social media and "review" sites (such as Yelp), where slanders often masquerade in the cloak of opinion. Why should then they be restrained in reporting an untoward activity in their neighborhood?

Because the aim of political correctness is to restrict our conduct toward others – apparently in order to preserve ethical conduct in society as such. Ethics, however, have many dimensions: the ethics of our family life, ethical economic exchange with others, ethics of different fields of human endeavor (environmental ethics, feminist ethics, computer research ethics, etc.), and the collective ethics of one society toward another. Every society also observes a different type of ethical system or system of values, which is intertwined with that society's religious makeup.

All ethical systems are concerned with our duties and moral obligations to the world. The personal, social, and political are often intertwined, and our particular religion merely establishes a "ladder of moral priorities" (e.g. the Ten Commandments). Christianity's main credo could be summed up as: "Help your neighbor" and "Do unto others as you would them do undo you." Eastern religions usually propound: "Learn to suffer and master your desires." Judaism: "Bide your time, observe the law and tradition." Islam: "The law of Allah is the only law. Spread this law and warn the world of the Judgment Day."

When the state begins to be concerned primarily with our ethics and morals, prescribing us how to speak and how to treat one another, it will necessarily encroach upon our virtues and our religion, because they are inseparable. In the attempt to secularize our ethics, the imposition of POLITICAL CORRECTNESS actually takes away our ethics and supplants it with – the State itself. The State is to be our God: the State prescribes us how to "help our neighbor" and "do unto others" and how to "observe holidays" and traditions.

This goes beyond just promulgating healthy laws, because – as far as the State is concerned – there is no God (!) thus no-one to whom our conscience could answer. Conscience does not matter to the State. What matters to the State is that you abide by laws and pay your taxes – and keep as silent as possible on the "issues of the State." In fact, our law prescribes that if you have no duty under law (for instance no duty to help your neighbor or, conversely, to report the untoward activities in your neighborhood), you should not undertake any effort to mitigate or even interfere with whatever is going on – because, by doing so, you would actually create and assume a duty (e.g. to help your neighbor) in a reasonable manner (or else you will be liable for negligence), or the duty to report something truthfully (because otherwise you might have to account for libel or slander in court).

103

We could seek solace in philosophy – but would we find it? In his Philosophy of Right Hegel strives to reconcile the modern society's concept of "social rights" (the rights we enjoy as members of a state and society) with "natural rights" (the God-given "inalienable rights"). Similar to Locke, he views social rights as contractual: we contract with the state for protection and in return pay taxes and respect our neighbors' rights to do the same.

Our "social rights" are delimited by ethical requirements of the society. These requirements are posed upon us by the social contract, which curbs some of our "natural rights" for the benefit of the society: my freedom ends where your freedom begins.

However, neither natural rights nor the competing "shadow rights" of the society should ever interfere with our conscience! After all, we are the country of Civil Disobedience and Common Sense. When a social right conflicts with any of the natural rights, the latter should prevail. When any such rights conflict with our conscience, it is our conscience which must prevail!

Political correctness may only propose guidelines which we may follow, provided our conscience does not object and our God gives us a blessing.

Of course, you have to have a conscience and believe in God in order to have the strength and skill to deal with political correctness.

In God We Trust

We must never forget this. We must never erase this motto from our shields. Why?

Trust is about faith. Faith is a moral conviction. As such, it is best cultivated by work, not by prayer. Work cultivates us and makes us strong. Strong men have the courage of persuasion. Strong men are courageous. Courageous men are not evil.

Evil is the product of weakness and fear. Fear is the father of deceit and violence. Many politicians speak about fear, some speak out of fear: fear of repercussions in their own party, fear of being scorned, fear of losing their warm seat in the House or the Senate…

Faith will set you free – not because you pray, but because you do your duty and follow your conscience. Slaves to a regime may have no conscience of their own – and none at all when their "masters" have none.

It is surprisingly liberating to abandon yourself to servitude: political or religious. It is easy because the loss of the pesky reproachful and suffering Self is perceived as a relief: relief from the pain of responsibility.

Like a child for whose negligent act the parent, supervisor, teacher must be held liable, so does a follower of an ideologue-demagogue or false prophet feel vis-à-vis reality. Alas, Faith is not something you place in "the other" – Faith is something you have within you, you treasure and show but never sell or loan or barter with.

How can you tell a false god, false prophet, or a demagogue from a real god, prophet, or statesman? The former will ask you to desert your Self and give away what you have for some larger abstract good, some generic idea of equality or humanity – or a "paradise" with virgins etc. He will ask you to abandon reality and enslave yourself to Him. Do you think that the conscience of this false Prophet is better than yours? Do you think that he (or she, indeed) has one?

On the other hand, a true statesman (though he may seem to act like a demagogue, because he will ask for your support and claim greatness in your name) will never ask you to forsake your soul and conscience for some abstract impalpable larger good. No. He will ask you to go home to your family, to work hard, be a good man or woman, mother and father, and help him restore the country.

Faith is a matter of persuasion in that what we do corresponds to our moral conviction. Every hard-working man is a man of faith. Struggle cultivates the Soul. If we persevere, work hard, improve within and provide without, we shall overcome our weaknesses and fears. Every human being has weaknesses but none is fundamentally evil. Evil, on the other hand, is fundamental in itself: it eviscerates the Good within.

I pity them who have been deprived of the Good within (their conscience, their Soul) by a false prophet. I pity them whose Good within has been eroded and rotted away by an ideologue or demagogue prophesying some imaginary "New World Order" in which we are all equal and there is no poverty and suffering. I pity them who have nothing left but void within, for it is that Good-less Soul-less void which the demagogue and false prophet fill and indoctrinate, injecting it with tenets of some false faith, perverted religion or political ideology.

Imagine what all those young men "fighting" for ISIS and praying five times a day could do for humanity if they studied and worked hard! It is harder to work and be a good human being than follow a "prophecy" and play with guns. It is harder to be an ordinary man or woman tackling the sufferings, pains and misfortunes of everyday existence, than rise above it all and, with a scornful grin, postulate a "New World Order." Do you think this false prophet – this "politician" – is a real savior? Like Jesus?

Who is like Jesus? Who truly partakes of the Savior? The ordinary man and woman who craves no fame. They who bring up their children to be good human beings, like themselves, and good citizens of their country: In God We Trust because we trust in ourselves and believe in our inherent goodness!

Ah, but being good in ordinary life is much harder than playing with guns, listening to an Albag'o'ghadi speak about virgins and paradise. It is much easier to forsake one's responsibilities and duties, and grant the prophet-politician power over you – the sugar-daddy Big Brother Allah Akbar power.

Why does the left not feel the need to define evil, set out a strategy and fight? This goes beyond Obama's sympathizing with the Islamic background on his paternal side. The general take-care-of-me mentality is the same in the left's secular world as it is in the world of religious fanatics who seeks some kind of allegiance, standing and recognition: Do I have to kill "to belong?" Do I have to cast blame in order to become a member of this party? Do I have to steal from "the rich" to be admired? Do I have to steal to win?...

But false prophets are not men (or women, in the context of Democrat candidates) of religion or persuasion. They might wear the cloth of the party, yes, but – change the background, change the circumstances – and you will tell the chameleon. As to the others: a veil over your face will not cover reality and a bandana and a mask on your head will not make you a brave warrior!

They call it "faith" because there is that void within, which begs to be filled. To believe is as human as to err. Do away with God and Christmas and you will do away with your humanity!

Terrorism is only a step further: it has already done away with humanity, self-reliance, self-love and self-esteem. They want to become "martyrs," because it is noble to "sacrifice" yourself for the higher good... There are two problems with this: martyrs die in order to prove a cause, make humanity better. One can think of Jesus as a martyr – or Socrates. No great dictator-prophet-tyrant or any of his followers have ever become true martyrs. Killing innocent people will not make anyone a martyr. It will make you a despised felon who will end up splattered on the street and your body? Well, no-one has claimed it so far...

Now, compare that to Jesus, whose drop of blood, shadow on a blanket, cup and everything he touched and said – are sacred and hollowed by us all. No, I am not a Christian, but I am a Human Being. As such, I have Faith. Jesus and Socrates are my heroes. They make me strive and fight, stay humble, yet aspire to higher ends, trying to become better every day. I do not pray – my whole life is a prayer! I am not religious, but: in God I trust.

The "martyrs" of totalitarianism, the "martyrs" of theocracy... they are the opposite of heroes. They are cowards, followers, weaklings. They shirk the pain and suffering of ordinary life, where true heroism lies. Pain and suffering are inevitable parts of human existence: we come to life screaming in pain and we leave it weeping and wailing in pain. The pain is never less – it is only up to us how we handle it and manage to fight the devil within which tells us to try painkillers, drugs, ideologies, false prophecies and gods. "They will set you free," the devil whispers.

"In God We Trust," we must respond; because we believe in ourselves and we know that we are free when we are free to fight our own pain and suffering first – without pointing fingers and blaming someone else or trying to succor someone else's weakness. "Ah, but life is hard," someone said to Voltaire. "Compared to what?" replied he.

In God We Trust. Without God, we are slaves: slaves to whims and fickle fortune, slaves to a demagogue, tyrant, false prophet... Yes, serving a demagogue is just as enslaving as serving a false prophet. Martyrdom is slavery above all others – it is nothing but fondness of death! Dying for a cause is only justifiable when you cannot live for one! Dying for a cause is only meaningful when it is not the end in itself, when you do it because you enable others to survive, when death is the means to life – when it does not foretell doom but gives birth and prevents destruction. Martyrdom for the sake of being a martyr does not come from faith or courage but is born out of fear and borne by fear.

No hero wants to be a hero. A hero wants to do the right thing when asked for help, when needed. A martyr – well, a martyr wants to be a "martyr."

Such martyrdom is Godless, immoral, full of sentiment, feelings for an "idea." This "idea" is not even an idea – it has become an icon, some untouchable miraculous image of Big Brother, Big Bagh'a'daddy who does not even inspire anymore – he only commands and you must obey, pray, obey, call slogans, obey and die! From a loss of perspective, from drowning in feelings, martyrs are born.

I saw a crowd of followers clapping their hands and nearly weeping over a demagogue. They were teeming with feelings: they shouted "I hate this and that" and cried out loud for "social equality, eternal peace and justice..." "We fight for peace!" they yelled, and: "Spread the wealth!" I saw them all too willing to give away their powers, freedoms, religion... Lost in the soul-less crowd, they turned into slaves and sheep. Their Faith? Their Conscience? That of the Demagogue...

I saw a crowd of followers raising their hands with clenched fists, crying: "Death to America!" and "Islam on Earth!" They too detest wealth and want equality – equality under one Tyrant. Lost, soul-less, sheep who would not recognize God if He knocked on their door.

Now, you might think, is that not noble and admirable, to cry so for a cause? Is it not noble to drop on the ground wherever you are five times a day and profess yourself a slave to the Icon? The ultimate cause is surely noble and grand: universal religion, world peace, world equality... Ah, I like ideas – you can do anything you want with them: you can scrap them, throw them away, you can realize them, improve upon them, make them into causes, and you can also rule over nations by ideas, with ideas, wielding them as swords – and killing with them too!

I watch them professing their faith. Yet, these followers of a noble "Other" have somehow, along the way forgotten about their own Souls, about the true God. They handed over their selves to the demagogue, the prophet, the one who subjugated and enslaved them on promises of paradise. They do not work – they clap their hands and shout slogans. They do not care about their children or their parents and grandparents – they kneel and pray five times a day to the "savior." They are but slaves. They want but to follow and die in their master's service.

Aye, it is easier to follow than to lead. It is easier to depend than to provide. It is easier to dissolve your Self in a crowd of weaklings, absolved of all personal responsibility. You must hand over the responsibility with your courage and moral persuasion – and feel good about it! It is like a drug addiction too because you "hand yourself over" to your prophet-demagogue and believe him (or her) that there will be no more daily struggle to live and provide – everything will be taken care of by universal equality and justice – or some magical transformation of the Self you lost into a soul in paradise…

Thus, ultimate weaklings are born every day, weaned on icons and images, bread on promises and taught how to become martyrs for a higher cause. Lack of responsibility leads to loss of conscience. Loss of conscience means no concept of morality. Good becomes evil, evil is seen as good. No-one even speaks of a justification, Mr. Kerry, because there is only one cause and all means are subjected to it. Evil is absolute.

"But I have my faith. I have my Allah, my Savior, my Demagogue…" they cry.

No, you do not! All you have is the empty idea, the bubble with you inside. All it takes is a needle-prick of reality and – whoosh! – you are gone!

Thus, when we say "In God We Trust," we mean (and do) much more than profess adherence to some religious tenet. It is the motto of our country, because all morality is founded on faith, and faith is more than sentiment, belief and abandonment. It means more than entrusting ourselves to the "other," whatever this "other" may be: God, Allah, Prophet, Politician. We must never lose ourselves in the flood of emotions produced by faith. We must never forget that it is the faith within not the faith without which makes us strong. When I enter a Church, I know that God connects with me because I have faith – He may give me courage, forgiveness, reconciliation... but not faith.

For US, common Americans in heart and soul, Faith is purposeful and pragmatic. It injects us with moral credo and ethical persuasion. We know well that if we improve, if we stay moral and good, if we fight for what is right and cultivate our inner courage and persuasion – not that of some prophet or preacher or demagogue out there – then we will have lived a meaningful life, life filled with love, learning and God!

That is where true happiness lies. That is our sole purpose on Earth. In God We Trust – because we are human and we believe that our exceptional, unique Country is, and always will be, the Land of the Free, the Home of the Brave!

Obama's Censorship:
Political Correctness Come Full Circle

During the horrific attacks in Orlando, the shooter called 911 and proclaimed his allegiance to ISIS. Under pressure, FBI released a version of the 911 "redacted" by the DOJ. AG Loretta Lynch made her "Rice parade" on Sunday, proclaiming on ABC and NBC that DOJ did not want to "re-victimize" those affected by the attack and that the matter was under ongoing investigation, which warranted "redactions."

The "redacted" version of the 911 call stated:

"I pledge allegiance to CENSORED. May God protect him. On behalf of CENSORED."

When something is scrubbed/deleted, it is not "redacted" but deleted, thus censored. We must be very particular about the meaning of the word. Redacted means adapted or changed in a literary form, not completely left out. Deleted means edited out. Clearly, when the information is left out, as was the case here, it is not redacted but CENSORED.

There is a specific use of the verb "redacted," which refers to a legal text with omitted personal details or other "sensitive" information, which is deleted in order to protect the privacy of the individual. Clearly, as the "un-redacted" text shows, there was no such reason to do this here.

Upon Republican outcry, the Attorney General of Social and Political "justice" Loretta Lynch, permitted that the uncensored text be released, which reads:

"I pledge allegiance to Abu Bakr Al-Baghdadi. May God protect him. On behalf of the Islamic State."

The fact that the name of the leader of ISIS and the pledge to the "Islamic State" have both been censored has surprised us all. But why?

I recall when I was growing up in socialism, there was no freedom of speech. One could not criticize the government. Any such criticism would be censored and the person prosecuted. Whatever information came from the West was also censored. No-one called it "redacted." There was no word-play anymore. However, the uncensored information was everything concerning the capitalist "evil" - what the socialist government called "poverty and misery of the proletariat in capitalist world."

The government (Socialist Party) was willing to delete whatever positive information about the "free world" there was, and preserve only the negative (market slumps, litigation, unemployment...), which it enlarged and enhanced, much like you see NBC do with whatever is uncomfortable to the Democrat Party today. By censoring (redacting, if you will), they thus created a new Evil, the Evil which had to be fought and conquered.

What is happening in our country today is the same in the opposite direction: by censoring Evil, Obama's administration is giving Evil a free pass. Evil becomes invisible – no-one may mention it, it bears a veil of secrecy, cover of political correctness. If you call Evil out, you are instantly accused of being a racist, bigot, homophobe, xenophobe, supremacist, even fascist. Meanwhile, the real Evil (which no-one in power dares call what it is - Islamic Fascism) is spreading like cancer.

The original "message" from the Orlando killer was:

"I pledge allegiance to Abu Bakr Al-Baghdadi. May Allah protect him. On behalf of the Islamic State."

The completely needless, willful and intentional substitution of God for Allah in the censored version released by the DOJ is more than censorship - it alters the meaning of the sentence! We do not have Allah on our currency. We do not have Allah in our pledges and oaths we say in court. We have our God - and to substitute one for the other is offensive and heretical.

There is more. When the information is not suitable to the socialist tyrant, he alters the meaning to make it fit his politics. God is mentioned not only in order to avoid all allusions to Islam, but also in order to project our Christian God into the context of this Islamic rant, thus making Christianity and Christian God the protector and guardian of Evil - and the bottom line of all the blame. Republicans, guns, Christians - are being blamed for an act of Islamic Fascism. Political correctness has come full circle – turning Good into Evil, Evil into Good.

One final note: if you think this is incompetence or effort to disguise Obama's failed policies in the war against ISIS, think again. Censorship is not about disguising - it is about manipulating. Every tyranny in human history has always started by manipulating free speech, censoring, redacting, showing propaganda films, printing texts skillfully fashioned to include a chain of information leading the reader to a particular conclusion. Censorship manipulates what we can say and - ultimately - what we are allowed to think!

"Pro-Choice" and "Economic Refugee"
Words That Should Be Illegal

Why do socialists like Sanders and Obama like to twist our language? The New Left is closely tied to the linguistic strain of prescriptivism, which started with Noam Chomsky. Words are not what they are – they are defined by their effects on your feelings. For example: "abortion" is a sophisticated, off-putting word of foreign origin. Socialists change it to "pro-choice," which makes it sound: 1) positive – it motivates the crowd to unite "Alinsky style" and follow; 2) it takes away the "fetus stigma" and focuses on the desperate woman, who is invariably alone, needing to lean on someone (insufficiency, dependence, solitude – is taken away by the icon-politician who suddenly rises as a husband-father figure and directs the woman to "march left-forward!"); 3) "pro-choice" also implies, by employing the preposition "pro" that it is PRO-gressive to go with the flow and forget about the past. Aborting a baby thus becomes of no more significance to the woman than dying her hair.

I cited "abortion" as an example only. However, you are probably not aware of the fact that IMMIGRATION AND NATIONALITY ACT \ INA: ACT 101 - DEFINITIONS \ Act 101(a)15P Sub.34 (which follows the definitions of an "immigrant" and a "refugee") defines abortion as one of the grounds for consideration for the "political refugee" status:

"[a] person who has been forced to abort a pregnancy or to undergo involuntary sterilization, or who has been persecuted for failure or refusal to undergo such a procedure or for other resistance to a coercive population control program, shall be deemed to have been persecuted on account of political opinion, and a person who has a well-founded fear that he or she will be forced to undergo such a procedure or subject to persecution for such failure, refusal, or resistance shall be deemed to have a well-founded fear of persecution on account of political opinion."

Of course not. Here, no-one in the "ruling elite" (or their lawyers, for that matter) will speak of anything other than "pro-choice." Thus, we accept women who are escaping "pro-choice" because they do not have a choice and offering them a new choice: "March left or go back where you came from!"

As to "illegal immigrants," Jorje Ramos will ask: "How can a human being be 'illegal'?" How about: when you are in the country illegally! If I enter someone's store after hours, I am committing trespass, arguably attempting a burglary. I will certainly be held liable because I was there ILLEGALLY. What is the problem the left have with this word? Let us look at what they are doing: by negating it or erasing it, they purport to say that the laws we have on the books – firm, well-thought-out laws, supported by a long line of precedents and legal argument – that these laws were created by some "old white men" to benefit themselves. They point at the Statute of Liberty and read the verse to us about "poor huddled masses longing to breathe free." As no-one teaches immigration or law in high school, 90% of Democrat voters will believe it: Oh, what a powerful image! What language!

Our country is a nation of immigrants, yes, but we all came here legally. Do you know what the criteria were for entry via Ellis Island? Immigration records date back to 1855. From 1892 to 1953, people who had any one of the following characteristics were sent back to Europe: 1) extreme poverty, 2) sickness, mental or physical weakness, 3) criminal record, and – mark this – 4) those showing any signs of religious bigotry or intolerance! That is what made us strong: the selection of the strongest, toughest, hard-working people who mean good and commit no evil.

As I write these lines, the left is proposing a new change of vocabulary: the "illegal immigrant" is henceforth to be called an "economic refugee." This was coined by two linguists – George Lakoff and his New Left pundit pupil Sam

Ferguson. An "economic refugee" is defined by them as someone who "seeks to escape oppressive poverty...because of global socio economic injustice issues." The core of this problem is that poor people want to come here to be better off. Economic refugee thus sounds correct – about the same as when we say "mentally challenged" for someone who is an idiot. Fine, we do not want to call people idiots.

In case of immigrants, however, we cannot automatically call them "refugees," because there are different types of legal status with pertinent requirements. The law distinguishes clearly between an "alien status" (depending on what is the purpose of the person's stay, e.g. athlete, entertainer, etc.), an "immigrant," an "asylum seeker," and a "refugee." An immigrant generally requires some type of visa. When we speak of a "refugee" we automatically waive the visa requirement. A refugee is anyone coming here based on a "well-founded fear of persecution on account of race, religion, nationality, membership in a particular social group, or political opinion." The law also expressly excludes: "any person who ordered, incited, assisted, or otherwise participated in the persecution of any person on account of race, religion, nationality, membership in a particular social group, or political opinion."

This is important, because if the so-called refugees cannot prove persecution, they are not legally refugees. They can only be immigrants, in which case they must have a visa, in order to be "legal immigrants." If they do not possess a visa, they are, by definition, "illegal immigrants." To call them "economic refugees" is wrong, and in itself not legal. This term simply legally does not exist.

The New Left is looking up to linguists and commands their lawyers to twist the law to fit their idealistic goals of curing "global economic poverty." It will not be cured by calling a spade a toothpick or a "shovel-ready job" a two-week salad picker who stays on social support and subsidies as a permanent "economic refugee" forever after. We do not need any grand new "comprehensive immigration

117

reform." We have had those in the past. All this funny adjective "comprehensive" means that it is thick, look scholarly, but no-one comprehends it, no-one knows "what's in it" – except, perhaps, the special interest groups and lobbyists with their pieces of pork... I bet they could quote page and line with respect to what "they got" in the new "omnibus."

No, we do not need new laws. All we need is an administration that will call a spade a spade and follow the laws we have: no ILLEGAL sanctuary cities, no ILLEGAL amnesties, no ILLEGAL IMMIGRANTS!

Oregon Farmers Represent US!

It was on a cold morning in the Fall of 1997 when I received my first CIA document. It was market "top secret" and I had to go to the Secret Service building in person, pass through two security "tolls" and sign twice, two separate documents promising I would not reveal the "secrets" I was going to be privy to. I carried that envelope as if my life depended on it... What a surprise it was to me when I reached my office and opened the file – only to see some gobbledygook about Oregon militias. Really? Was the Czech Secret Service really interested in this? Why?

Well, post-communist Europe was trying to copy the United States in everything: the bicameral representative democracy, the system of checks-and-balances... Why the United States government was interested in some armed farmers trying to protect their land was something I did not contemplate or question at the time. The information could not possibly have been of any use to the Czech government. It was not my business to inquire into the subject matter though, and – you know how it goes with these "top secret" documents – the sooner you forget, the better. I would have never thought, not in my wildest dreams, that those ten or fifteen pages of incoherent descriptions of some men allegedly "training" in an Oregon forest would ever come up again in my life!

We all remember Concord and Lexington where the militias rose up against the British oppression. Militias are basically "all able-bodied men over the age of 17" up to 64. Yes, all such men should have guns and be able to participate in their states' "unorganized militia" training or whenever called upon by the governor. Militias were originally to provide for our common defense, because there was no standing army at the time, which was of utmost concern to George Washington, who was well aware of the drawbacks of militias in terms of military skills and organization. Two days before his death, in a letter to Thomas Jefferson, George Washington urged that a military academy be founded to create a standing army. He is the father of West Point – and the rest, as they say, is history.

Not so fast! Militias continued to play a significant role in the war of 1812, the Civil War, and pretty much all other wars we have ever waged. The only problem has always been organization, command, and sometimes also willingness to serve for long periods of time. After all, militia men are fathers, sons, men who have families and have to make a living…

In 1903, Theodore Roosevelt, issued an order to state governors to "keep militias 'in check' so no more than several hundred would be in training and on the ready in any state at any given moment." Why? Did he fear common men would rise against their government? It is also not coincidental that Theodore Roosevelt declared the area where today's stand-off in Oregon is taking place a National Wildlife Preserve in 1908 (a reservation for migratory birds, that immediately moved to the tilled farming land for food and nesting; and for Indians, although there had not been any at the time and have not been any since). Thus, he took this land from the people, appropriating it for the government. Why? Because land means power, independence, liberty! Since 1908, our Federal Government has been steadily expanding – which also means taking more land from the states.

The men who took over the Federal building in Oregon are farmers with guns – the so-called "unorganized militia" (10 U.S.C.). They are sometimes referred to as a "reserve militia." In other words, they are the descendants of the men who stood up in Lexington and Concord against the British and fought valiantly for our freedoms whenever they were under assault. Remarkably, during the Civil war, Oregon, Washington, and California were significant providers of unorganized militia forces for the Union – supplying infantry and cavalry both to resist the Confederacy and suppress civil disorders caused by the secessionists, Copperheads, Mormons, Native tribes...

The Harney Basin where the Hammond ranch is located was settled in the 1870 and, by the time President

120

Roosevelt established "Malheur National Wildlife Refuge," local ranchers were grazing over 300,000 head of cattle on this land. The Hammonds bought the ranch in 1964. Since the 1970s the Fish and Wildlife Service (FWS) along with the Bureau of Land Management (BLM) have been forcing them out, buying adjacent land, revoking permits to graze, and making their lives miserable. Nearly every farmer succumbed to the pressure and left – not the Hammonds. In spite of all the hurdles cast their way by the tax-paid apparatchiks, they continued to care for their land and cattle.

We all know that farmers have to "burn" the land to increase health and productivity. It is done all over the world since 5,000 B.C. The Hammonds put the fire department on notice of such annual "burns" in 2001. In 2006, it helped save their home and prevent the spread of wildfires. It probably saved the state and federal governments significant amount of tax monies too. Instead of being grateful, federal agents arrested them! The judge found this absurd and released them with nominal reprieve.

Five years later, in 2011, they were arrested again! Mr. Hammond and his son were sentenced to five years as TERRORISTS under the Federal Anti-Terrorism Death Penalty Act of 1996! Their home was raided by the federal agents, exonerating evidence disappeared, the Hammonds' attorney was given restricted access to evidence (1 day - the Federal prosecuting attorney Frank Papagni had full access for a week), and "witnesses" were brought in to testify against them – one mentally challenged, the other did not know anything about the farming customs of burning and tilling the land... Consequently, the Hammonds were found guilty, fined $400,000 and received a "minimum terrorist sentence" 3mo (father) and 1year (son). They duly served their sentences and were released.

Upon their release the Federal Prosecutor Papagni went on a crusade, appealed to the 9th District Federal Court, and had the Hammonds return to prison for 5 years! Imagine this breach of double jeopardy and cruel and unusual punishment taking place against a member of BLM! The son, Steven Hammond is 46, has a wife and 3 children.

His father Dwight is 74. He has to leave his wife Susan after 55 years of marriage! If he survives, he will be released when he is 79.

This is a generational feud of the people v. the government – Dwight Hammond's father, Steven's grandfather, died of a heart attack during the previous litigation. BIG COUNTRY! Where is Hollywood? Sucking up to the administration? It is also worthy of note that US Attorney Amanda Marshall (who made the recommendation to challenge the Hammonds' original sentences) resigned in May 2015 for "health reasons" amid a scandal (accused of stalking a subordinate).

When the power is taken from the people, when the justice system becomes corrupt, when all other measures fail – where can the people turn? The power of the people rests in the vote, their security in the militias. Thanks to our President, the "organized militias" are now facing the "unorganized militias," very much like the Democrats are facing the Republicans or – even more poignantly – the political establishments of both parties are facing the rise of the people. Wake up! Those farmers in Oregon represent US, the United States of America, against ALL dangers, domestic and foreign!

What Is Ideology?

It is my premise that not only is the ISLAMIC STATE based on an ideology, but that this ideology is familiar to all of us and intersects with ideologies that warp and waft our own society. This analysis shall be prerequisite to defeating any similar anti-cultural, anti-civilizational movement each and every time it reoccurs in our future.

Through Hegel, Marx, Bell, Kojeve to Fukujama, we can follow the development of the modern concept of "ideology" not as a "science of ideas" (Idea + Logos) but as a system of beliefs to which we have ripened throughout history, being forced to accommodate our ideas to reality. By WE, I mean people, society as "political animals." The latter term is Aristotle's and means literally "zoon politikon," that is "an animal capable of thinking" ("zoon") and "an animal tending to congregate and form a society or polity."

Such analysis and rationale remains no more than a restatement of our own dichotomy: our metaphysical selves (our dreams, emotions, hopes) will always try to combat and conquer our Reason. Every IDEA is devoid of that (part of) reality which it does not need: when I imagine a beach or dream I am on a beautiful island, there will only be the people I want there to be, no litter or shards of glass, crystal clear water without seaweed, the sun will always shine and a pleasant breeze will be gently fanning my face. Well, this is an idea. This idea is devoid of the elements of reality I consider unpleasant or superfluous.

When an idea is implanted in your mind from without, we may refer to it as a "received consciousness" (Marx's term). A demagogue or ideologue or social organizer will attempt to implant this "consciousness" *en masse* and *in toto* – turning it into the received consciousness of many, thus forming a conceptualized version of the IDEA which is referred to as an –ISM: communism, fascism, racism, terrorism – but also capitalism and liberalism – are all conceptualized systems of beliefs based on a central IDEA.

The latter two may be considered positive because they fundamentally transform the individual from within in a positive, aspirational way: similarly to a mythical hero, the CAPITALIST HERO follows his dream and ventures into the unknown in order to establish his enterprise. He goes to the woods and comes out with a basket of mushrooms or a bearskin. He will face a pack of hungry wolves along the way and befriend a lonely fawn. In a CLASSICAL LIBERAL HERO will go against the society in order to reform stale social norms: he is laughed at and disparaged, but eventually persuades the whole village that, in order to kill Beowulf, they must cooperate.

The former conceptualized idealisms (communism, fascism, ISIS) are not based on an individual heroic transformation (coming from within) but on a mandated *en masse* transformation from without. They approach polity (society/village) from the point of view of an anti-hero whose primary goal is to destroy everything and return to some point in the past – be it the Empire, Reich, Caliphate – when society was "ideal." This "idealized" (romanticized) society requires personal sacrifice: either in the form of total self-abnegation or actual physical self-destruction.

There are two immediate problems with both positive and negative conceptualizations: the problem of ANCHORING, the term I hereby coin to name the inherent human aching and craving for a "status quo" which would set up the ISM-society as permanent; and the problem of JETTISONING, the term I have established for discarding the elements of reality which do not fit the central idea (usually because they question or contradict it, thus leading to its overthrow or destruction by rationalization).

If the IDEA is sufficiently strong or sufficiently deeply "received" and implanted into the individual consciousness of every "zoon politikon," the ISM-society will be established as "permanent." Fukuyama pointed out that this permanence will always be under assault from historical "events," but that all societies ultimately aspire to a worldwide LIBERAL DEMOCRACY. When the world has thus "evolved," time will "end."

124

Derrida assaulted this notion as neither original nor valid, because coined by the French philosopher Kojeve, the dichotomy between the history-as-event and history-as-state is derived from Hegel. As Schopenhauer noted, the idea was that of Kant, who merely played around with the Platonic terms for what we know about what we see. The IDEA we hold is a noumenon but cannot be the thing-in-itself. Realism is thus no more than human craving for reality. We can see the chair but can we KNOW what "chairness" is?

The IDEA is never fully attainable. We may conceptualize it and reiterate that a capitalist economy founded on liberal democracy is the best system of government KNOWN to Man. However, as such, it remains a noumenon (the thing as we want it to be, name it and perceive it as such), not a phenomenon (thing-in-itself – the "real thing" which always entails corruption, human vices, selfishness, etc.).

Both "liberalism" and "democracy" have been subject to multiple interpretations in the past nearly two hundred years. Fukuyama's final "end of history" cannot be a *status quo,* because this state will be composed of fluid noumena. Further, Kojeve, Feuerbach, Lacan and other interpreters of Marx (and Freud) tended to do away with the dichotomy between God and Man by "overcoming" God – in the new liberal democracy, God is superfluous because Man is complete in himself. This is the same secular peace of the soul that Hinduism and Buddhism achieve by meditation and Islam, apparently, by violence.

The final outcome is not that of some radical assault on capitalism but the statement that capitalism in the post-historical phase (Kojeve's term) has been transformed into liberal democracy. This is still an IDEOLOGY, however, and the proponents of modern liberalism will not consider it complete and successful until they finally do away with all the limiting requirements: that of language, borders, even currency. The aim of the ultimate ISM is to construct a borderless society with one currency where all languages and cultures would merge or communicate on an equal footing. For the lack of a better term, this ISM-society would be referred to as LIBERAL DEMOCRACY.

Note that the terms: LIBERAL + DEMOS + CRATOS are all positive, based on positive ideas – those of FREEDOM and RULE by the people. Most modern Marxists view direct democracy as an inevitable part of their communist-socialist ideal. Our nature favors them, because as human beings, we tend to overlook the negative and focus on the positive: hope is always the last to die, even after courage and other virtues are long dead, Hope is still hanging by, uncertain what to do, awaiting orders from the "master consciousness," from above. Liberal democratic "social order" is stronger than any other because it is based only on positive IDEAS. Yet, ideas they are, devoid of all unwanted or undesirable elements of reality.

How is it possible that some fundamentally negative –ISMs have taken over societies and ruled in their own right? Take ISIS, for example, which is both a totalitarianism as well as a theocracy (government whose laws are religious and whose rule is by and through a system of fundamentalist religious beliefs). If it were only a totalitarianism based on rigid hierarchy and subjugation, or only a religion based on priestly obeisance and genuflection to the edicts of the church, it would not survive. Totality is parasitic of religion and vice versa here. In other respects, its aims are identical to those of the modern liberal democrat: borderless society with one currency under one "noumenon."

As we do not naturally tend to base our individual system of beliefs on an apocalypse, death, end of the world, suicide and destruction, we can clearly see that these (negative) ends are not ends in themselves but means – means to a higher religious end whose tenets serve a higher purpose, thus can be PERCEIVED AS ethical *per se*. Religious ethics do not permit questioning.

This rationalization is more difficult when the means (presented to us as ends) are positive: such as global peace, community of nations, one government always knowing what is best for the people. As we cannot properly

126

see the end-in-itself (the thing for what it is – a caliphate for the totalitarian rule of the world, liberal democracy for a stage on the way to worldwide communism), we easily become swayed and deceived by propaganda.

Thus, the secular ends of these fanatics are often achieved by the means of sacral symbols and sacred propaganda with rites and indoctrination into what is presented as a special secret society (covered faces, black robes, secret codes). We must never forget, as Joseph Campbell stated, that our conscious self is always subservient to our subconscious: once the hero enters the forest, he is forever transformed. Once the anti-hero kills at the order of the gang-leader in the "acceptance ritual," he is likewise forever transformed.

In "primitive societies," this transformation led to understanding and unity with God. Where "God is dead," this transformation leads to further estrangement from oneself: the society of diverse people propagating diversity fosters strangeness and otherness. There is no more a Self but only the Other. The mirror tells us not who we are but who we want to be for the others who want us to be something for themselves, something else than we are by nature: queerness of gender being one example, forced acceptance of all immigrants, especially of other faiths and races being another.

What is more, our rational self can also be converted by argument, as we all know from advertising and commercials. We are often persuaded to purchase what we do not need or would never have even wanted to try... Likewise, a practicing Muslim can be rationally swayed by the power of ISIS' advertising of a new caliphate, new state, new world order serving their religion above all others. He will be seen as an archeological find which must be destroyed – unless he joins them NOW. Why? Because everything old must be overcome. The new world order is post-historical and post-ontological and post-eschatological (meaning: it is after "being" and after "history" – has overcome both).

Further, such a word order is compared to the previous social system, which was either that of (e.g. Assad's) oppression and tyranny, or that of democracy where their religion was merely one of many, but certainly not the dominant one. Who would not want to be a member of the master religion, master class, master society...? I would venture to go so far as to state that most people first persuade themselves of the benefits of this "new order" TO THEMSELVES, and only subsequently toe the line of the outside coercion and indoctrination which merely supports their already existing belief and thus exists only just to "stabilize" the society, set up the "status quo" of this destructive order.

Thus, most Syrian immigrants (technically "emigrants") will remember Raqqua as a small Paris, a beautiful city where they grew up – and will long for it as such. On the other hand, most of those who stayed behind and joined the NEW ORDER of ISIS, will see the "new Raqqua" as better than the old one, which survived in a different totalitarian regime, in which they were not the ruling class. The militant ones, who have infiltrated the immigrants or who have traveled to IS and back in order to wage Jihad abroad, in those the rational "weighing" of ideas central to their ISMs (previous and current systems of government) is suppressed by the metaphysical ends (the ends of destruction) which are to be means to the ultimate end of ABSOLUTE LIBERATION, which may only come from death.

Religion provides us with the ability to reconcile ourselves and accept death as part of life. Religions in general do not treat death as a goal but as a transformation. The soul undergoes purification or reincarnation (Samsara). Technically speaking, RADICAL ISLAM is "radical" because it takes the transformation literally. Whenever you forgo the metaphor and interpret the Holy Word in a literal sense, you are not reading what God (Allah, Buddha, as the case may be) wanted you to read. What is more (and, on this point, both Hegel and Kant see eye to eye) Reason will always want to grasp the thing-in-itself, but will always be one step behind because reality is too large, insurmountable by Reason itself, because what we can absorb is inherently limited by our being only human. If we do not understand our inherent human limitations, we will always be subjects and slave to our cravings and desires. In a larger sense, the IDEA of the –ISM will absorb us and rule us, depriving us of reason.

It follows that ISIS adherents are too immature to realize that the paradox of their suicide is glaring: they do not kill themselves as Diogenes did, by the force of WILL upon the MATTER (Diogenes is said to have forced himself to cease breathing), but by an order from the above: given by their "comrade-superior" in the totalitarian hierarchy and, at the same time, propounded as the ultimate "ideal" by their theocracy. Their absolute liberation thus means absolute slavery, enslavement which ends in death. Reincarnation or purification is impossible because they die by suicide, killing others, which is an inexpiable sin in all religions known to Man. Therefore, RADICAL ISLAM is not a religion – it is a cult.

In many cultures, death in combat is a mark of honor. One may think of the Japanese Kamikaze pilots. In many cultures, subjugation of the masses is the ultimate goal of the master-class. However, in no society which we call a "culture" is destruction perpetrated upon the unarmed innocent populace – so called "soft targets." President Obama is correct in that the "society" they have established is ultimately self-destructive, as are all totalitarian regimes. Unfortunately, we cannot wait for another fifty years nor can we go through the sacrifice of another fifty million people. What is more, our natural propensity to hope and absorb the reality of the world by our noumenal classifications (political correctness) may eventually be equally self-destructive.

Finally, how does a "culture" of an –ISM turn into a cult? By transforming its central IDEA into an IDOL. In Christianity, Jesus represents an idea – the idea of goodness, charity, equality, friendship etc. For RADICAL ISLAM, Muhamad represents an IDOL. For the true believer, he is no different from Stalin, Castro or Ceausescu.

However, the IDOL is neither God nor a man. The IDOL is a man-made representation of the idea. It is once removed from noumenal reality and twice removed from phenomenal reality. It is the lowest form of worship which does not bring happiness but slavery – slavery to the Master who created the IDOL and all its other metaphysical representations, such as all aspects of a totalitarian government.

The only "post-historical" system of government would be a government completely absolved of all ideologies. Meanwhile, since we cannot live without an ideology, we must beware to always keep it in check and balance the good against the bad – because if either one prevails completely and forever in any ideology, it will kill us all.

On Principled Conservatism

Principled conservatism is often presented as the opposite of moderate conservatism, also called "malleable" or "flexible" because it adapts to the requirements of our times. Thus, Donald Trump is allegedly not a "real" conservative because his views are "malleable." On the other hand, Senator Cruz is always principled and unbending.

When I say that I am "conservative," what I mean is that I like my habits and routine. As a political conservative, I have a strong moral persuasion (not necessarily of a particular denomination), I do not like experiments with society, I do not believe in free "stuff," and definitely disdain governmental apparatchiks with their intrusions into the way I live and do my business. In brief, I am a conservative because I love America and capitalism. I want to mind my own business and want everyone else to mind theirs.

In general, what defines us as conservatives is the belief in small government which is a necessary evil and should intrude as little as possible into the Pursuit of our Happiness, founded on achievement and personal property, wherein our liberties are anchored. When the government is taking away our rights and property, tyranny arises. Many conservatives would also state that God, Marriage, and Pro-Life are the doctrines they espouse.

The overarching component of conservatism is national security, powerful military and respect for the police force, many of whom are military veterans. As long as these principles are above all others, we are willing to consider more liberal measures, such as social support for the truly needy or immigration quota provided refugee status is legitimate and there is proper vetting (the person is not just a freeloader coming here to use US or do us harm). Is healthcare a right? No! Is education a right? No! Is a certain income a right? No! You get as much as your work is valued by the market – and you can buy as much healthcare and education as you can afford. That is conservatism.

This may sound harsh but it is decidedly more fair than government redistribution of wealth and property, which always leads to cronyism, creation of a privileged class, and fear of the individual vis-à-vis the mass. Why? Because the individual does not matter – only the State does. Imagine what a nation of one billion slaves, such as China, could do if they had a real democracy and real market economy – not one fiddled and fudged by the Party higher-ups. Imagine how happy and strong people in Iran would be if they did not live in a totalitarian theocracy but a country based on individual rights and achievements!

We live in a country founded on principles, the key one being that all people are created inherently equal. Thus, we can only differentiate ourselves through our own efforts, and not by the means of "redistribution," i.e. what someone gives us or what we (or they) steal from someone else. America is the best country in the world because all true Americans (excluding socialist "AINOs") know that money is a byproduct which represents hard work – it is a gift back from the society to the individual who worked hard and thus deserves the means to purchase property, healthcare, education... Government is useless where market is at work, because all of US speak through the market, not just a select few "experts" or what-difference-does-one-human-life-make-anyway apparatchiks.

Yet, I sometimes find myself wondering whether the so-called "principled conservatism" does not go too far: whether our unbending Faith, the idea that the institution of marriage is between a man and a woman only, and abortion is a sin – whether all these basic percepts of principled conservatism do not hold us back from unifying as a country and being stronger than we currently are. What Carter called "malleability" of Donald Trump and Beck his "populism" are precisely the facets which differentiate Mr. Trump from "principled conservatism" – and which may enable him to win a general election.

On the one hand, one should never be so adamant and principled as to be stubbornly closed to the outside world; on the other, one should never compromise one's principles if it should change our moral and ethical core. For example, to protect life in all its forms is a fundamental principle anchored in our Declaration of Independence as well as our Constitution. When in doubt about the meaning of the Law of the Land, we ask the Supreme Court for clarification; but the High Court does not always seem to "get it right" – and we are left wondering why.

Take Roe v. Wade. This 1971 "trimester based" decision, which balanced the woman's right to privacy (unstated in but supposedly implied by the Constitution) with public interest of the baby, created two camps of unhappy campers. Justice Scalia was one. The Supremes revisited the issue in PP v. Casey twenty years later, deciding, on a more "sophisticated ground" that if the fetus is able to live outside the womb, it enjoys constitutional protections. Common sense tells us that there is something decidedly wrong with such a way of thinking, if only because it has to be judged on a case-by-case basis. Roe was perhaps better, because of the balancing test, but even that decision undermines our deeply held belief that all life is sacred.

Atheists may smirk – until one of them has an abortion only to find out that she can no longer become pregnant. There is more: you will never stop asking yourself – what that child would have been like today; or there may be another child who will always miss that slaughtered sibling… and that lack, that lacuna, that gap in your life will be there till you die! With regret, you will realize that no-one is truly "unwanted" and that every human being is capable of love, if love is given to them. Why! Conservative principles stand on thousands of years of human experience and wisdom!

Nonetheless, for political purposes, in order to compromise and give to God what is His and to Cesar what is Cesar's, we must distinguish between contraception and abortion, marriage as a church institution and a state sanctioned contract, and we should understand atheists as people in search of moral principles. Unfortunately, they are often misguided, ill-taught and swayed by the power of the

State. If so, it may happen that they will relinquish their freedom and bid Cesar to perform what only the Lord can.

I grew up as an atheist in a country which despised religion, where the only God was the State. It was much harder to find rationale and justification for the Good as opposed to Evil in life, and to tell them apart. It was not impossible, with a lot of reading and self-discipline, but where education was government indoctrination and history was purged propaganda, the only truth there was lay in fairy tales, Greek myths and legends – and philosophy. We possessed a few smuggled books, underground truths spoken by the brave: Havel, Skvorecky, Klima... aye, even Orwell found a secret path to my bedroom.

People cheer for a "revolution" today because, although they have free access to undiluted history and information, they do not read and educate themselves. No free college or university will do the work for you! I have known many a Ph.D. as cold and spineless as a curvy and scaly reptile... They had been educated by those state-sponsored universities, you know. Revolution? Once there is a "revolution," anarchy follows, violence is the product of anarchy. BLM sheep whine about the "police state!" Alas, my friends, you who grew up in this wonderful most powerful democracy in the world, you have no notion of what a "police state" is. It is a state without any personal rights. The only right you have is to keep quiet and toe the line!

We are a country of laws, but we are also a country of principles. You can live by the law and be a good person, but you can also be sentenced under the same law – because the judgment of the law is not a moral judgment. It is a judgment which weighs the interests of one party against the other, often society versus the individual, such as in the abortion cases mentioned above or in eminent domain issues or in every criminal case, where the people (society) sues the individual for an act against the people. It should be our aim to align our laws and our basic moral percepts but this cannot be done if either party remains close-minded.

We must understand that it is sometimes for the greater good to give up our property for fair market value in order for the state (people) to construct a road. Conversely, all people must understand that the powers of the state should never outweigh the rights of the individuals which delegated these powers to the state. Morals begin at home – not in college, university or with the imposition of laws and state powers! Immoral individuals will not be "made moral" by the state. Only moral individuals and personal influence – and love – shall prevail. Therefore, this weighing of "public interest" should start not in the courtroom or on a political platform, but in each person's heart and mind – for the Nation is only as strong as the sum of individuals that compose it.

In conclusion, principles are not wisdom, but lack of respect for principles is ignorance. Can there be a "principled ignorance?" Only when you know what you do not know and can distinguish between the two, as Confucius said – but then it is not really ignorance, is it?

Diversity Is Longing for "the Other"

Diversity is a natural result of globalization. However, Globalization is meaningless if it does not unite Humankind for a common purpose. Diversity must come naturally – or not at all. Artificially imposed diversity weakens a nation, it does not make it stronger.

To follow nature means to obey God. Unfortunately, our public schools avert from all forms of catechism and laugh at God. By ridiculing religion, liberal atheists are turning away from not only their origins, but their very substance – religion is extremely important for every human being's mental health and equanimity. If you think you are too "scientific" and too "smart" to believe in God, allow me to remind you that Albert Einstein believed in God, as did Isaac Newton and Aristotle... How does that make you feel? It should make you feel humble and inquisitive, not pompous and condescending.

Indeed, religion is important as a founding stone on which culture is built. However, it cannot be just any religion in any society. A society which rejects its religion – in order to tolerate all while having none – is volatile, internally weak, susceptible to being attacked both from within and without. When atheism reaches the point of no return, the individual feels empty, abandoned, unloved. This translates into the feeling of the society at large. Civilization suffers. If you deny the existence of God, you are unable to accept true love and forgiveness.

Being empty within, people either start to crave for their roots again, or reach out to the dominant nations and their religions. The first is a historical and philosophical process: we crave not just for our constitutional founding roots, but also for our past leaders, our legends and myths. When religion disappears from our lives, myths must take its place, in order to sustain social structure and cohesion. Recently, we have seen it with the re-emergence of Star Wars, fighting the imaginary enemy, an inter-galactic monster, a many-headed dragon in the form of saucers and robots. You must not offend the fans – "It's a religion," they say. True. A myth re-unites the society and fills individuals with their proper "social function." We exist not merely to create and pass on our individual heritage but, above all, to foster and reinforce our nation, to further our culture, to support our civilization.

All our national mottoes express this culturally unifying function, stimulate us as individuals to persevere in our small pursuits and deeds, in order to create one great America! New Deal, Great Society, Yes We Can... Every time we come in contact with a foreign culture, we try to be tolerant, but we cannot be tolerant of the "other" which never accepts US, our culture, our religion, our myths and legends. When I hear CAIR attacking our system of laws, suing an employer over "Muslim prayer breaks" for employees (settled in *Pickering v. Board of Education* (1968) 391 U.S. 563), when I hear the Mayor of Philadelphia stating a religious killing "in the name of Islam" had "nothing to do with Islam..." I wonder whether the Americans who stand by in silence or even further such outrageous acts of forced assimilation by "doing as they are ordered" (in the famous words of an infamous Dachau supervisor) know what they are doing?! Sociologically speaking, they are committing genocide upon our culture!

Whenever in history a society and its culture was in crisis, people turned to religion. When religion failed to support them, fairy tales and myths rose into prominence. People would also inevitably turn to their governing bodies, their chosen, appointed or elected "heroes" to stand up for them in times of need... Where are they now?!

The reason why young atheists in the ranks of Sanders-Clinton followers do not see the cultural emptiness they have been thrown into is because they were told State stands for God, and there is nothing the State could not do: take property from one, give it to another; take guns or allow them; dole out money, forgive debts, refinance mortgages, regulate markets, provide for the poor of the world...

"What does 'your God' do for you?" they will ask. "Look at what Obama can do!" They will pause at our silence and say: "Your God can't stop ISIS! But Obama – at least he is doing something…" But what?? Those youthful idealists have never really suffered, they have never known real poverty and never been subjected to the rule of a dictator. It is the suffering, the poor, the sick and oppressed that always turn to God – and, unlike Obama, God is always there for them!

In our materially rich, spiritually poor world, we are trying to revive the great minds of the past: Hegel and Marx on the left; Kant, Locke, Hume on the right; Aristotle and Plato on both sides. However, it is not the works of these thinkers that we read, but interpretations or snippets of wisdom and quotes, 140-character Twitter "treatises" with Facebook links and u-Tube "sources." Only the tip of the iceberg comes up on the screen. The soul, the heart… they remain empty.

With this emptiness, this demise of one's own religious and cultural roots, the insatiable craving for "the other" arrives. What follows is the assault on language: deconstructing texts, creating "narratives," complaining about "the tone." Politicians dabble in our language as if it was a cake they themselves are not too eager to eat: a nip here, a poke there… Perhaps "my people" will like the marzipan, the politically correct façade? What they are doing is smuggling "the other" into our language. What they can, they erase (e.g. the word "nigga" in Mark Twain). What they cannot erase (e.g. the word "terrorist") they ban: all of a sudden, it is a "T-word!" Raping the English language, they are molesting our culture! What is our culture but the mother who gave them birth, weaned them from pups! It is a crime too atrocious, whose consequences I dare fain to contemplate…

The "other" is something we want to revere, in order to fill the void within left by God. Thus, populist demagogues come and go, trying out their grin-and-gaggle on us. Of course, some will always fall for the front, because the absence of God makes the human being shallow. Character cannot mature in shallow waters. Those who have fallen for the ideologue, to them, the Ideologue is the deity, and nothing will change their minds. If Sanders says this about the Wall Street, then it must be true. Sanders' word is their commandment.

What they do not see is that economic conditions are only manifestations of inner spiritual life, which means God within: faith in oneself and love for one's country. As they do not believe in God, they are empty inside. Their economic struggle is conditioned by their spiritual emptiness, and reflects it in their conduct, which is that of a herd of sheep, not autonomous, independently thinking individuals. Before you go without and scream mottoes and follow your populist demagogue idol as if they were a god, you ought to pause, turn within yourself, and reflect upon what lies beneath the crust, the façade, the marzipan on the promised paradise.

Needless to say, "the other" may be represented by a culture or religion foreign to our kind. We are accepting of many other religions and cultures today. It is healthy to the extent to which they bring us positive charge, health and wealth – cultural, social, and ethical growth.

Nevertheless, should we be void within, lacking of our own culture and tradition, faith and persuasion, should we not fight for what is truly ours, not stand up when assaulted and maligned – then we would become that herd of sheep at the mercy of an idle shepherd, the idol inviting foreign gods (or prophets, if you will).

What is more, an empty person has nothing to offer in the cultural exchange. When one culture murders, rapes, kills – with the ultimate aim of destroying all other cultures – and the other culture stands idly by, following an idol, it is the latter which will be destroyed.

Our relationship to other cultures should never be that of submission and dependence, but that of reciprocity. The "other" must accept US as we are, on reciprocal terms. The "other" must not be forced upon us, but we must both go and meet each other half-way, for equal benefit, be equally willing.

One example for all: the "meeting" of the Buddhist, Hindu, and Christian cultures: every Friday, by the local pool, people with Indian heritage don their traditional gowns and costumes to dance and cherish and revel their culture.

They are peaceful, innocent, welcoming. You cannot not admire and love it! Those ladies look so splendid, with stars adorning their foreheads... it is like a fairy-tale! Of course, on "normal" weekdays, you would not be able to tell: in all other respects, they are Americans! This is multiculturalism.

There will always be emotional strife and struggle, bickering and bartering – that is human and fosters civilization. What stultifies it is killing by suicide-bombers, torture, rape, mass murder... Whenever such actions occurred in human history, they were doomed to spite and ultimately failed – but not without a fight, Mr. Obama, not without a fight!

Interestingly, these "cultural relapses" have always occurred prior to a religious renaissance. Christianity had had this period during the 15th and 16th century. Witches were burned in Europe until the 1750s, roughly about the time we declared our independence. After the centuries of Dark Ages, blights, plagues and terror, a new era began. No wonder it has taken another 300 years for a less advanced religion, stultified by totalitarian rule. Civilization travels from East to West. It reached China and India half a century ago, and now ... Iran and Iraq.

The search for the "other" is at the same time the search for the meaning of life. Today, we believe that the meaning of life can be grasped, described, photographed, stored on the computer and reviewed in detail. However, all such depictions are only interpretations. At school, children learn interpretations. Consequently, later in life, these children will become adults used to taking shortcuts by means of interpretations. Gullibility is built into our education. Snippets of reinterpreted "wisdom" surround us. Turning on Twitter is passing through waters, seeing tips of icebergs, rowing on, propelled by the desire to "connect," to be a part of humanity. Has internet substituted God? And what happens to such youth when they have no God within, no firm moral and ethical roots? What happens when they feel lost, when they cannot shout "USA! USA!" without offending someone – when they "do not belong...?!"

Then the search for the "other" ends in disaster: drugs out of desperation, gang-life out of the need "to belong," ISIS or Starwars (?) – out of the starving Soul! We cannot accept – and will not be accepted by – the other when we ourselves have forsaken our God and remain empty within. That calls for scorn and dominance, which is what Islamists are showing our atheists. At the same time, inner emptiness is not a civilizational but a human dilemma, which is why "our" western youth may sometimes look admiringly at ISIS as "rebels" who want to undermine and overthrow our entire civilization. Their undeveloped minds are not any less or more developed than those of an average youth in our western societies. It takes the experience of everyday struggles for a human being to become "ripe" and appreciate life. Clearly then what connects "our" atheistic idealistic youth and the radical Muslim murderers, is the desire to follow the idol. It is a vacuous and vain desire, which emanates from emptiness within. In the absence of God, they long for something – anything – without.

We have taught them how to substitute religion with Hollywood – legends, myths, fairy tales transformed into a modern setting. However, the veneer of computerized tricks and professional fly-jumps and shoot-outs is all too clear to penetrate. One must be capable of "keeping up the pretenses," fostering one's own imagination, belief in the supernatural – before we abandon ourselves to a moving romantic movie or a dramatic chase James Bond style...

There is a strange connection between religion and imagination – one fosters the other. It is a healthy symbiosis, which produces moral and ethical human beings, capable of overcoming suffering and becoming what God wanted them to become; or, for those less "religious" out there: to follow their bliss. In order to follow your bliss, you must believe. Thus, happiness and belief are inseparable.

Social stability comes from the absence of inner and outer conflicts. Multiculturalism is a way of achieving it. Mutual understanding and respect is at the core of Judaism, Christianity, Buddhism, Hinduism... Such civilizations flourish. We ask forgiveness and respect to be respected. We do not slaughter to "earn" a place in Paradise.

Finally, the search for "the other" may result in lack of finding either: a religious root within, outside, without, or a substitute supplied by Hollywood or modern technology. Such a person will remain lost and shall not recover unless helped, set on the right path. All too often, it is these lost souls that opt for painkillers, drugs, crime or suicide. Even some psychosomatic disorders may be seen as effects of inner spiritual emptiness: chronic depression, fibromyalgia, compulsive and manic disorders, gender dysphoria... These are often "scientifically" medically analyzed and causally interpreted. The main causal factors, however, are impalpable – they lie deep in the soul of every individual. The good old saying: "The doctor treats but only God heals" answers all.

What is society like when those who search for "the other" find only such "other" which is equally empty and hungry within? It becomes a society without a state or nationality. Nationality consists of language, morality, religion – even borders are secondary to our language and religion. Empty society is running away from itself, asking for shelter and food – as if God and Faith, belief in oneself, were qualities as palpable as bread and water! The unsatisfied becomes insatiable, asking for more: more and better – food, house, car, money from "the rich..." They look outside for help, thinking more multiculturalism will help – more like us...

But what is US? Is US the Other?!

Radicalization from Start to Finish

How does RADICALIZATION start?

RADICALIZATION is a process of becoming an extremist, one who follows an idea which is attractive to him or her because it is "winning" and speaks to their inner selves. It is – a calling.

RADICALIZATION is a process which penetrates the human soul from two directions: from within, and from without. It is a process we all know very well. We have all been radicalized in certain respects: I am radical about what I read and watch. I am radical about what I eat and drink. I am also radical about how I think about politics and ideology – because I grew up in one and know it close and personal!

RADICALIZATION is not any different from our "conversion" to some activity we love: I love to swim, so I join the team, we swim together. We are keen on it and feel a familial bond when we get together and compete. It springs from within because we all need some form of persuasion, some grand and noble idea to follow. It is one of the greatest and noblest of human characteristics. As such, it is also supported from without, because there are already followers and societies that accept us as their members.

RADICALIZATION can be good and productive if it is based on an idea which advances humanity. Edison was a radical, so was Ford and Rockefeller. To think of it, Jefferson, Hamilton, Madison, even George Washington was a radical – rebels, mavericks, radicals all! RADICAL means strong headed and persuaded of one's own right and of the value of what one says and does. In a way, Donald Trump is a radical – except his RADICAL PHILOSOPHY is that of America First, and it does not kill or hurt anybody.

RADICALIZATION is not something one is subjected to and must accept. I grew up in a society which wanted to radicalize me, make me into a communist, blindfold me to the Free World. I was taught communism, I had to wear a communist uniform, go to communist manifestations where I was supposed to shout: "With Soviet Union Forever and Never Any Other Way!" The more they forced it into me, the more I resisted.

What happens today is no different. It takes place online and in mosques but there is little difference in terms of its appeal as an IDEOLOGY. By being secreted, it is made even more attractive. People in the West are RADICALIZED precisely because they are not forced into it the way I had been. They find it appealing as a CULT and an IDEOLOGY.

ISLAM is not a religion of peace for one simple reason: it is not able to defend itself against this RADICALIZATION. The majority may be "peaceful Muslims" but they are but followers. It is the RADICAL MINORITY that rules and prevails, because they are the leaders, they set the direction of the whole "nation" or "House" of Islam, if you will, in the same way the communist "papalashe" set the direction for entire nations when I was growing up.

The only way TO DEFEAT RADICALIZATION, and thus radical Islam, is not to trace every single convert and look for needles in a haystack! The only way to defeat them is to make the ideology itself unpopular, not cool, unattractive – and show that it has failed or that it leads to nowhere. This must be done: 1) by eradicating them physically (not here but at the root), 2) by having stronger propaganda, 3) by ostentatiously displaying our cultural superiority.

First, physical eradication. This is clear and requires very simple strategy, a pincer maneuver supported from the air. Untie the hands of our military and they will do the job in a week or two. Just cut them loose and let them do their jobs.

Further, do the same with the police and FBI at home. Let them choose the means and ways, and let them "profile" if they deem it necessary. Profiling means composition of details into a picture. For that, you have to be a great fact-finder. Modern detective work started with

144

Sherlock Holmes and if you can say one thing about Sherlock: he was a great profiler, detail and fact-finder.

Second, propaganda is a concerted media effort, which must begin by promulgating our uniqueness and pointing out disadvantages and drawbacks of the typical Sharia society, which is a backward totalitarian theocracy and for which there is no room in a civilized society. We all can contribute to the blogs like this one and make ourselves heard in a persuasive way.

However, the main propaganda must come from the government. Perhaps we should have a propaganda center within the CIA whose purpose it would be to only make movies, videos, write blogs and post well-informed, targeted internet propaganda.

Third, we should all fly American flags – not just at home, but abroad. I would swamp the Middle East with American flags, pictures of Hollywood and little bric-a-brac souvenirs showing our American greatness. I would do the same with all media in the Middle East. When I was growing up, the Russians were constantly jamming Radio Free Europe and BBC World Service. Instead, they were feeding us pre-digested, censored "news" about the greatness of the Communist World. There's a thought...

When President Obama called them a "JV Team," he was right in one respect: they are inferior fighters with no military education, and they are also too inexperienced and young to know what life is really about. Someone who believes in "Paradise and 77 virgins" is mentally undeveloped and intellectually retarded.

Finally, the House of Islam must stop teaching Quran literally. NO RELIGION is to be taken literally. ALL RELIGIONS are allegories and guides to our lives. There may be real elements and stories in them, but the substance is to guide us to a productive and peaceful existence. To paraphrase Hayek: it is always the most painful experience when we find out that the ideal we have blindly followed led us to the very opposite we wanted to achieve. In this case, two misguided Muslim fanatics ended up splattered on the street like road kill. They will be buried in shallow graves

145

where no-one will visit them but a stray dog that will go there to mark its stone. Paradise?

Finish. The END of RADICALIZATION.

Democracy, Amnesty, Citizenship
and Anchor Babies

It is 500 B.C., Athens. Cleisthenes took power 8 years ago. Seeing that there was a continual strife among the ruling clans, leading to tyranny, he changed the tribes by taking away their family names (patronymics) and turning them to the names of the places they came from, after the local peoples (demonymics), divided geographically. This socio-geographical "gerrymandering" enabled the first "sortition" – elections based on ability rather than heredity. Each "demos" (geographical people) was represented. True democracy was born.

Cleisthenes established a court system where jurors were equally selected from each demos (tribe or polity, if you will). Everybody was equal before the law, equal at the polls – thus, he called this system iso-nomia (iso=equal, nomos=law). Any citizen who was deemed to have too much power was exiled. Such tyrant-to-be could retain his property but was unable to be physically present and influence people.

In order to be a citizen and have the right to vote, one had to be born in Athens. This became known as the "law of the soil" or "Jus Soli." Greece was still a relatively small, unpopulated country and almost everyone lived in Athens. When Rome began to grow into an empire, the old Greek "Jus Soli" had to be first extended to all the territories of Rome. This was done by edicts, proclaiming the citizens of the conquered lands also the citizens of the Roman Empire, thus subjecting them to taxation and Roman Laws (for example: Edict of Caracalla).

The other device for expanding Roman citizenry was the "law of the blood" or "Jus Sanguinis" – making all those born to Roman citizens elsewhere (e.g. the Gaul, Britain) Roman citizens at birth. This was based on the blood relationship, not the relationship to the (Roman) soil.

The edicts making new citizens (mentioned above) are not comparable to modern amnesties by executive

147

action because Roman Empire expanded, people were not physically moving and immigrating (to Rome or other parts of the "old empire"). The empire expanded to them.

Only one citizenship was possible, only one allegiance recognized. However, this also had undesirable effects, such as making it more difficult for Rome to recruit soldiers and increase the number of legions because prior to the edict (of Caracalla) being issued, there had been conditions on acquiring citizenship, one of them being that the new male Roman-to-be had to join the army and serve (in order to deserve citizenship).

As there were different periods of expansion, so there were also different levels of incorporation of territories and peoples (somewhat akin to the acquisition of territories and their recognition as states in our history). Citizenship had different levels with a different scope of influence. Only Cives Romani, full Roman citizens had all the rights: to vote, to marry, to sue on contracts, to bear arms... basically our Bill of Rights, Roman version.

One could achieve higher status as an immigrant by staying in Rome and working to improve the state. Granting citizenship to allies was also a great step forward in the "Romanization" of newly conquered territories and a powerful political tool. Alexander the Great successfully "mingled" and assimilated Persians, Egyptians, Syrians... under one heading.

This idea did not survive him very long, but it seems to me that our effort in Iraq was very similar – until recently. Post-World War II arrangement of Europe into "zones of influence" was also based on the same old (Alexander's) devise of ruling over foreign nations.

Today, we recognize both: the law of the blood and the law of the soil and apply them so as to maximize our population. There exists very little discrimination and the only "level" of citizenship is that a person not born on the US soil (Jus Soli) cannot become the President or function in close hierarchy thereby (Vice-President, Speaker of the House, Chief Justice).

The only other difference is that between a permanent resident and a full-fledged citizen. Green card gives you the right to travel, do business, work, and reside on US territory – but not the right to vote. It should also not automatically grant you constitutional rights and protections.

If there should be indiscriminate right of citizenship (by executive action, i.e. edict or amnesty), then we have to re-institute the old Roman "levels of citizenship." The right to vote should stand above all others, and be granted only to those citizens who have no other allegiance (no double citizenship) and have been in the country for a period of years, contributing to the economy. Any form of the dole, social support and almstaking from the government on the part of these newly integrated citizens should disqualify them from voting. Language proficiency in English ought to be a must, for how can you vote if you know not what you are voting for?

Currently, there is one level of citizenship and constitutional protections and rights are granted across the board, which is NOT FAIR to the native United States citizens who have lived here, worked and paid taxes and those new citizens who have done so for a major part of their lives.

The right to citizenship of so-called "anchor babies" is based on Jus Soli, not Jus Sanguinis. It is not necessarily older than Jus Sanguinis, the right of blood, which goes back historically to primitive exogamic tribes and, later, royal lineage and intermarriage. The problem with any kind of right is that once granted, it is difficult, if not impossible, to remove. As the right to citizenship under Jus Soli, the law of soil, it is legally gradually extended from the anchor to the entire family, even if they live abroad. The system is absolutely open in this respect, which incentivizes foreigners to come here just to give birth (to "throw the anchor" on our soil).

Let us be mindful of the origin of the word: the Old English "ancor" borrowed Latin "ancora" and Greek "ankyra" means a "hook." The figurative sense is that of stability and security" – also securing people together (television "anchor"). Thus, we cannot speak of anchor babies unless we also speak of anchor-families, extended "tribes" of people anchored by Jus Soli. We can drop the "babies" and merely use the word "anchor" for it has a more substantive meaning on its own.

How is this problem approached by other countries? Great Britain chiefly implements the right of blood – at least one parent must be a British citizen. The right of abode grants citizenship to those with sufficient ties to the community, similarly to our residence rights in a particular state of the Union. The right of abode, however, is more difficult to acquire. In fact, there are many levels of citizenship: a "full" British citizen, born and residing therein; a BOC or "British Overseas Citizen" (Malaysia, Kenya – with the right to travel and do business); British Subject (British India or the Republic of Ireland); BNO or "British National Overseas" (people from Hong Kong and China); and BPP or "British Protected Person" (neither British nationals nor aliens but people with ties to the Commonwealth). The system is not foolproof but it protects Great Britain from foreign self-serving intrusions.

In Germany, until 2000, the right of citizenship could have been acquired purely on the Jus Sanguinis basis – in other words, one parent must have been a native German citizen. As of 1/1/2000, at least one parent must have had permanent residence for at least three years and been residing in Germany for at least three years.

In France, Jus Soli applies indiscriminately, which makes me think that perhaps our Jus Soli has been influenced by French laws, which, until recently, stated that anyone born in France or on former territories of France may automatically request French citizenship.

Coincidentally, as Bill Clinton finished his second term as President of the U.S., he could have claimed citizenship of France and run for leadership there under the law passed in 1961 [Article 21-19(5°)], which enabled people from former French territories to apply for immediate naturalization, bypassing the normal five-year residency requirement for would-be French citizens. As Clinton was born in Arkansas which had been part of French Louisiana before it was sold to the US, it was held that he would qualify under this law. Therefore, as a naturalized French citizen, he could run in the French presidential election.

Clinton himself later repeated this claim in 2012 as an amusing thought when speaking to an interviewer (http://www.businessinsider.com/how-bill-clinton-could-be-president-again-2012-9#ixzz2UWa3XxQL). However, by then, this possibility had already ended, because Article 21-19(5°) of the Civil Code was repealed (by article 82 of law 2006-911) on July 25, 2006 under the direction of Nicolas Sarkozy, then Minister of the Interior.

France currently makes a child of a foreigner French citizen at the age of 18, provided that the child resided in France since age 11 for at least five years. Younger children may become French citizens if they have resided in France continuously for at least eight years. Five years of "habitual and continual residence" is required for naturalization, as is the case in the United States.

As an attorney practicing in the area, I see very little room for improvement in the United States' immigration system. Requirements for knowledge of English should be increased and rights obtained by family relationship limited. Permanent residency (Green Card) should be available to all those who have not been on (any kind of) government or social support for the past five years, have continually resided in the country and paid taxes for the past five years.

Laws applicable to minors in France (see above) would well behoove us to apply domestically too. Stateless persons, refugees, people willing to serve in our military – should all be approached with certain advantages. Many of them already exist and are applied. Finally, in none of the countries stated above is citizenship granted at birth unless the conditions posed on the parents at the time of birth are met.

Natural-Born

Article 2, Sec.1, Clause 5 states:

> "No Person except a natural born Citizen, or a Citizen of the United States, at the time of the Adoption of this Constitution, shall be eligible to the Office of President; neither shall any Person be eligible to that Office who shall not have attained to the Age of thirty-five Years, and been fourteen Years a Resident within the United States."

Under Article 1, Sec.8, Clause 4 of the United States Constitution, Congress establishes the rules for naturalization. We all know that "naturalized" is not the same as being "natural-born." Simply put: you are natural-born if at least one of your parents was an American citizen at the time of your birth.

However, the issue is more subtle. The subtleties began with the passage of the 14th Amendment and continued throughout our history. Donald Trump is correct that whenever the law is in any way unclear, it is the High Court should interpret and determine what Congress meant. Had our Constitutional interpretation been strictly pursuant to the rules of "Originalism" and "Founder's Intent," (propounded by J. Scalia and Hugo Black) we would face fewer problems than we face now, with the structuralist and contextualist interpretations introduced by the New Left, including political balancing of interest (which modernly started with J. Frankfurter).

We all recall that the question of what "natural-born" means was hotly debated during President Obama's candidacy and pretty much ever since. It was not as thoroughly analyzed and settled as it should have been. It keeps coming up with respect to the so-called "anchor babies" and their rights under "jus soli" or the Law of Soil, which dates back to the ancient Athens. Jus Soli grants constitutional rights as citizens and nationals to all people born on the U.S. soil (including the right to vote). Under Jus Soli, Senator McCain is a US citizen because he was born on a naval base (a sovereign US territory), but Ted Cruz would not have been, because he was born in Canada.

Both parents of Sen. Cruz were US citizens, however. Historically, it is arguable whether the Law of Blood (Jus Sanguinis) stands above the Law of Soil (Jus Soli): I am not aware of a case where a Roman general's wife giving birth to a child while stationed abroad would not have given birth to a Roman citizen – mostly because Romans considered the whole world their territory and because pregnant women about to give birth would not travel outside Rome. Why? Because they wanted to assure that their children would be citizens of Rome.

We may trace the combination of Jus Soli and Jus Sanguinis to the Ancient Greece. In my view, the Greeks were more advanced in that a freed slave could have become a citizen of Athens, and a child born to a slave would have. To the Romans, on the other hand, all slaves were disposable chattels with no rights. Anchor-babies would have stood a better chance of becoming citizens of Athens than of Rome.

Similarly, what lies at the core of Mr. Trump's argument is the combination of Jus Soli and Jus Sanguinis, which is applied when someone is born outside the U.S. territory. As of November 14, 1986, such a person becomes a "natural" U.S. citizen (as opposed to a "naturalized" citizen) if, and only if, the following criteria are met:

1. The person's parents were married at time of birth;
2. One of the person's parents was a U.S. citizen when the person in question was born;
3. The citizen parent lived at least five years in the United States before the child's birth;
4. A minimum of two of these five years in the United States were after the citizen parent's 14th birthday.

Senator Cruz clearly meets items 1 and 2. As to the third requirement, it is generally interpreted as follows: the citizen-parent must have lived in the United States for at least five years at any time prior to their child's birth. There may be some room here for the argument that it has never been settled whether the five-year period must be consecutive or if it can be counted cumulatively, and whether the five years must immediately precede the birth of the child or it could have been at any time after the age of 14. However, in conjunction with the fourth requirement, it becomes clear that the five years could have been at any time between the age of 14 and the birth of the child. What is more, only two of the five years must have been after the age of 14.

Had clause 4 not been present, President Obama would have been in trouble because his mother was 18 when he was born and thus, by definition, could not have lived in the United States for five years after the age of 14. It should have been examined if she lived continuously in Hawaii (US soil) from 16-18. We know that she traveled to Indonesia and possibly Kenya during this time... What is more, this law applies to persons born after 1986. Prior to that date, the requirement was that both parents had to be US citizens. As President Obama was born prior to 1986 and his father was a citizen of Kenya, it still remains to be seen if his presidency has been legitimate. If not, Congress should either make an exception or adopt a resolution "legitimizing" him as President ex-post-facto or – ...

No such problem arises for Sen. Cruz, however, whose mother was in her 30s and did reside in the US for at least five years after the age of 14. Either the High Court or Congress can shed more clarity on these conditions by defining whether the 5 years are intended as "cumulative" or "continuous" and what exactly is meant by US soil. If, for instance, an ambassador's wife stationed in Paris has to briefly leave the embassy (US sovereign territory) and go to a Paris hospital, does the child become a natural-born US citizen?

Obviously, any intimation that a foreign-born national (God forbid with an accent!) should become our president is off-putting, especially to conservatives. But, ask yourselves, would you rather have a president who is a Constitutional conservative, excellent US lawyer, patriot in all respect, standing up for our values and Bill of Rights – or would you rather vote for a "first-generation" natural-born socialist? Why should the latter be more of a citizen than the former? Isn't that un-American?

I am full well aware of the fact that I am not "natural-born." I may note this with a smile, but it does grind against my American Heart and Soul that I shall always be a "second-class citizen." To console myself, I recall Albert Einstein, Felix Frankfurter, Madeleine Albright, Henry Kissinger, Arnold Schwarzenegger... Did they mind? Well, I think they did – but we still think of them as accomplished men and women, great Americans. After all, the People of the United States have the power to recognize a "naturalized" citizen as "natural-born" at any time – by a Congressional declaration of "eligibility" as to the particular person (Art.1, Sec.5), by means of legal interpretation from the Supreme Court – or, by a Constitutional Amendment.

I know it sounds far-fetched at this point, but such an Amendment may be desirable in future. Many smart, patriotic legal immigrants have come to our country and it may happen that one of them arises to the position of running for the office which requires that the candidate be a natural-born citizen...

We are an exceptional country. Our democracy is still young and, in many respects, fragile. Imagine: your great-grandfather may have fought in the Civil War! While Europe stands still, looking up to us, we are running forward with our Torch of Freedom, making progress for Humanity – truly – in leaps and bounds! Let us always do what is best for US, for our country and our future. If Ted Cruz had been born on Mars, I would still want him over the US "natural-born" Bernie Sanders!

Is Donald Trump a Demagogue?

Glenn Beck has just stated that Donald Trump is a demagogue and that he (Glenn Beck) will not vote for him if he is the candidate. So Donald Trump signs a pledge and reaffirms that he is a Republican and will not run as an independent, thus endangering the outcome of the elections, but when the table has turned, the others cannot say the same – that they will support him?!

With this attitude, Mr. Beck and those like him – all "honorable men," all "principled" Republicans – may find themselves living in socialism!

"Demagoguery" is native to democracy. Demos (people) + agogos (to lead) is what a politician in a democracy does. The profane version of "demagoguery" is the result of dozens of political leaders in the history of democracy (since ancient Greece) who have abused this power, i.e. the power invested in the people with which WE THE PEOPLE vote for our favorite leader. A true demagogue lies and deceives in order to foster his or her private autocratic ends. A true demagogue cries "Fie!" at a debate and calls for violence and revolution. A true demagogue is not someone who swears allegiance to a party and supports conservative ends!

As "demagoguery" is native to every democracy, the difference between a statesman (a good demagogue, who wants to further the good of the people and make the country great) and a politician (a bad demagogue who wants to rule and dictate) is therefore twofold: that of a degree, and that of orientation. The one who goes over dead bodies, goes for the revolution and wants to upset and undermine (transform) current social order or status quo, such a politician should be called a "demagogue." A real demagogue is a community organizer who uses a pretext (such as race) to gather people into a voting block. They do not vote based on persuasion (rationale) – they vote based on an emotion which has no rational basis. One who votes for Clinton because she is a woman has already given the power of the individual to a dictator.

The one who simply feels the same desire to change the trajectory of the economy and foreign policy in order to revert and stabilize the country – he is a not a demagogue but a statesman! Have I just called Trump a statesman? You bet! Everyone on the GOP stage last night was a statesman (one was a "states-woman" but I am sure she would not mind being called a "statesman" either). Even Bernie Sanders is a statesman because he truly believes what he says. He is not lying to achieve some secret autocratic ends. Of course, he does not understand that the ends he believes in will lead to tyranny, but that is a different matter.

Democracies fall as they rise – by the power of the people. Therefore, WE THE PEOPLE must **never give away that power** lightly. We loan it to the best candidate who we trust will turn the tide in our country's, our family's, our personal benefit. We must never say we will not vote because the person on the ballot is a demagogue. That would spell the end of democracy. That would be the shortest way to hell – in our case – socialism.

European Migrant Crisis:
The Worm Is Squirming

Even as Angela Merkel is inviting more refugees to come in, refugee camps are being torched and random Muslims attacked in the street. About 10,000 migrants are arriving in Germany every day. In view of the changed naturalization laws and universal social and medical care, most intend to stay. They are refusing assimilation, refusing medical care from female staff, even turning down the food they are provided for free. As one of the thousands of fighting-age Muslims said: "Give me my money! I want my money to buy what I want!" The money he speaks about is the 3000 Euros of German taxpayer's pay into the treasury, which has to pay approx. 11 Billion Euros for the refugees this year, mainly for free medical care and shelter. A refugee summit held by the German parliament in July budgeted 5.6 billion euros for an expected 450,000 asylum applications this year. In light of the recent mass influx, however, Germany is now expecting to take in some 800,000 by the end of December.

Processing and administrative fees, accommodation, meals, pocket money, health costs... are part and parcel of this deal, which majority of German citizens rejects. Both Social Democrats and Conservatives warn against the "suction effect," such as when A. Merkel decided to accept thousands of migrants who were "stranded" in Hungary. Germany is 70% Christian (slightly more Catholic than Protestant), the rest are atheist. I wonder whether atheists are actually more accepting of a fundamentalist religion like Islam, which makes no distinction between religion and state (theocracy)... and, yet, they too have seen the hordes of young Muslim men shout: "Allah Akhbar!" in front of the train in Hungary. When Hungary attempted to closed the border, they threw stones at the police...

They are called "migrants" by the local European peoples because they think these "migrants" do not intend to stay. The notion of a "migrant" is deep rooted there – while that of an "immigrant" is virtually unknown (unlike an "emigrant" – someone who ran away from oppression). Many other wars have striven Germany and Austria since the Muslim siege of Vienna in 1526 and then again in 1683. Even before, there were wars and migrants though. All children across Europe are taught about the "Great Migration" or "Migration of the Nations." I believe it was in the third or fourth grade in elementary school that we had to memorize the weird-sounding names of Goths, Vandals, Lombards, Angels and Saxons who settled the east, central, then westernmost parts of Europe. Later, the Huns, Avars and Slavs came, in constant strife and struggle among themselves as well as against the Moors, Turks and Mongol tribes, always viewed as (our) enemies...

It was the fall of the Roman Empire resulted in splintering and national uprisings. Every time an empire falls, there is a search for separate cultural identity among the many peoples who were part of it. It happened again with the death of Charlemagne and again with the demise of the Habsburg Empire. Now, it seems, European Union is in danger of disintegration. The Ottoman expansion, which lasted for centuries, survives in history books and the minds of school children and only political correctness of the United Nations prevents local politicians of expressing their justified fear of what might happen, of what is happening...

German immigration and naturalization laws were greatly relaxed in 2000 – prior to 2000, nationality was based entirely on *jus sanguinis* (blood relationship); today, children born on or after 1 January 2000 to non-German parents acquire German citizenship at birth if at least one parent has a permanent residence permit and has had this status for at least three years and was residing in Germany for at least eight years. Further, since 2006, Germany has a National Integration Plan and Charter of Diversity. This year, the total influx of Syrian, Eritrean, Afghan and other immigrants to Germany is about 1% of German population (800,000), nearly three times as many as during the crisis in Yugoslavia.

Turkish people (not very well distinguishable from and certainly sympathetic to the current illegal immigrants) have lived and worked in Germany for years. Yet, they have never fully assimilated. Native Germans still complain that they "stink" (smell differently) and do not know what "hard work is." They had started coming to West Germany during the 1960s and 70s, the so-called "Economic Miracle" years. Just as some argue that we need laborers from Mexico, Germany had been in need of factory workers. Many of the Turkish citizens did not want to become German citizens and would send money home and return to Turkey even after they had relocated their families to Germany, for vacation and to maintain their properties there.

It has been a while since I lived in Germany. It was nearby Frankfurt, a small village, streets so neat and clean you could eat from them. The whole village looked like a beautiful colorful congregation of gingerbread cottages. The houses were so well-kept and maintained that I felt an instant need to touch the façade, the way you touch clothes in a store: what a shock compared to where I came from, cold, gray, dark and dilapidated communism. Some houses here even had colored gravel, pink, blue, yellow...

Inside, every household had 6 color-coded trashcans (paper, plastic, cans, glass, wood, garden waste) and every day its precise clockwork order. My friend Karl, son of my mother's friend, who had emigrated to Germany shortly after the Warsaw Pact invasion of Czechoslovakia in 1969, invited me to his room. His father was German and he, of course, likewise.

A guitar was hanging on the wall, a poster of some pop-music group was taped to the door, clothes over the couch... a typical realm of a typical teenager. After a while of getting to know each other, he reached on his desk, shoving off another book, and showed me a neat leather copy of Mein Kampf. He was grasping it like I would an Anthology of American Literature or the Bible itself.

Of course, Mein Kampf was banned in Germany at the time. Still, everyone had one at home, he said, although they would not talk about it in public. I was unimpressed. It is a very poor book and has never been praised for its intellectual or spiritual qualities. However, simply the fact that it was banned was enough for people to get it. It must have more of a symbolic meaning... that of guilt and expiation, as Karl Jaspers would say.

I did not think twice about it, but it was probably a mistake. In two days, we drove to Nuremberg with his father who was looking for a particular store to buy wood from for his business. We were slowly passing by an old building which resembled a castle. I asked about it. Silence. Karl turned to me with the index finger on his lips. I blushed. Whatever conversation we had had in the car till then, was suddenly over.

Later, when his father left the truck, he explained to me that we had just passed by the "Palace of Justice" and that no Germans speak about it out loud. I felt like I made a faux pas, but could not take it back. I asked no more, but it was made clear to me that anything concerning World War II and Hitler was a conversational taboo with the Germans.

All this is swallowed with a timid smile. It has the cold, bitter taste of Octoberfest beer. "Better drink and forget," locals say. Deep within, the proverbial worm is squirming but has not "turned" yet. "When" is the question, I believe, not "if" it does...

Nothing Ever Happens

So there you have it: ambassador Stevens wrote more than 700 e-mails requesting aid, Ms. Clinton deigned to less than 70 responses over the critical one year period. No help came. He and three others died in a senseless, predictable and fully avoidable attack! I am no decorated general but common sense tells me that if you require military aid, there should be direct communication with a military center, circumventing all political centers.

It also does not escape me that Secretary Clinton's ex-post-facto conduct was fully in compliance with Alinsky's Rules for Radicals: "Pick the target, freeze it, personalize it, and polarize it." The video was a fine target – a person of ill repute who made it, for whom no-one cared, was a great Alinsky scapegoat. The blame and responsibility was quickly shifted to the target, which was frozen, personalized and polarized as a politically incorrect racist extremist.

Like all governmental apparatchiks, Secretary Clinton is also fond of using the passive voice, gerund and participle: "The action was being taken," and "it was communicated," etc. Language without a subject is language without a person. In grammar, we call this an "agens." In practical life: the government speaks, therefore responsibility for actions spreads like thin vapor over the Walden Pond… What remains?

The Benghazi "scandal" is a fine case in point on how the government works: from the top down, and if you want to communicate something, you must go begging and pleading, hoping someone "up there" will here you. Let us say you want to implement a change. Let us say you have been granted a budget to develop a project (as I was). You want to execute your task as fast as you can, with maximum efficiency, as if it were an important examination. You want to present the project fast, build a name. It is your little brain-child, the result of your toil. You hand it in to where you have been directed, to your immediate superior (sub-head of some sub-department in a compartment of a department).

Then: you have to wait. You are paid for waiting too. You may just as well enjoy it.

However, you keep waiting and waiting and waiting… Nothing happens.

You see, nothing ever happens, because the government consists of departments. The departments have sub-departments with sub-sub-departments. Each of the department has its separate hierarchy and a staff. You have to start from the lowest apparatchik of the staff, present your product, paper, project – whatever it may be – and rely that they will pass it on to the higher apparatchik in the chain, eventually to the head of the sub-sub-department, sub-department, department, Secretary's Office…

The problem is that by the time it reaches the sub-sub-department head and goes on to the next department, eventually reaching the secretary of the secretary, so much time will have passed that either the issue will no longer be actual or the budget gone or both. Have you read Kafka's Castle? How about the Metamorphosis? If you have just started working for the government, those will be the stories of your life…

I speak from personal experience. When I was working on the White Book Project of primary and secondary legislative terminology at *Directorate Generale* 1a in Brussels (DG 1a was the EU Ministry for Associated Countries at the time), I was "given" (promised upon final approval) a budget of 25mil Euros to execute the project of translation-interpretation center for EU legislature.

I did everything I was asked to do speedily, but I also needed a final go-ahead from the Minister of Foreign Affairs in Prague. You cannot imagine how difficult it was to get through the bureaucratic machinery and obtain the final decision. It would have been easier to see the Queen of England!

I wrote dozens of faxes, letters, made phone calls… all in vain. Finally, I faxed a brief letter addressed to the Minister of Foreign Affairs in Prague, indicating that I was going to accept the grant myself and implement the project as an independent entity, a private business. Wow! I had my response overnight!

The Prague Minister called the Brussels Minister who invited me to her office for some "red carpet treatment." She looked stern, attempted a smile. We liked each other from our prior contacts and she was a little upset I did not go to her first for advice.

"I have received an info from your government relieving you of your responsibilities," she said. It took a while to break the Czech brick of ice which landed on her desk, but she did: "We have to be patient, all of us. There is a rigid hierarchy. It is frustrating, I know, but that is how governments work," she paused, "especially in 'your' country."

My "immediate dismissal" was suspended and I completed my term at the European Union. The money fell through, the project was never materialized though. Governments do not care about such spits in the ocean as 20-30 million. Unless you speak in billions, you are not speaking Government.

My point is: how can anything happen if everything depends on so many people up the food chain and no-one has any ultimate responsibility, no-one ultimately cares if anything happens? Those who want a warm office post with all the perks grin and bear it. Thank you very much, I'll pass.

Regulated to Death

It often amazes me how blasé and unconcerned people are about the system they live in. I did not grow up in a democracy, I can never take it for granted. The government shall not collapse under its own weight – people will! The power of the individual decreases in direct proportion to the increase in the power of the government.

Can you think of one aspect of your life which is not regulated by the government? From the moment we wake up and wash our face (water regulation), put on the light (electricity production and use, regulated by FERC), the car emissions, the air we breathe (EPA), roads we walk and drive on (FHA), facilities we use... to the moment we come back home and turn on the television set (FCC) – it is all regulated by the government, even the food we eat! Finally, when we die, our burial falls under state and local funeral regulations – how and where to "dispose of us" is carefully regulated by both the federal (FTC) and local governments.

The United Nations Statistics Division (UNSD) classifies multiple functions of a government. This classification is descriptive, meaning it captures the functions governments currently fulfill. As to the United States, our federal government overlaps the states' governments and where they collide, the federal prevails over local (Preemption Doctrine).

UNSD classifies the functions as follows:

1) General Public Services (economic)
2) Defense (military, civil, foreign)
3) Public Order and Safety (courts, police, prisons, fire dept.)
4) Economic Affairs (commerce, labor, energy, agriculture, transport)
5) Environmental Protection (waste management, pollution)
6) Housing (water supply, street lighting, community amenities)
7) Health (hospitals, medical services)

165

8) Recreation, Culture and Religion (sport, culture, broadcasting)
9) Education
10) Social Protection (disability, VA, sickness, housing)

As we can see, even these divisions overlap. Thus, we have to pay taxes to several departments (doing the same thing) which probably do not even communicate with one another. Some areas should not be included at all (such as religion) and others should be greatly simplified so as to promote personal individual freedoms and free market economy, not government planning and bureaucracy!

The government is obligated to publish all changes and new rules in its "Journal" called the Federal Register. This journal includes all new and proposed regulations, requiring the affected companies and individuals to comment on them within a certain time period (30-60 days). When Rep. Issa proposed a modernization of the Register (March 11, 2014), his proposal met with strenuous opposition from the American Association of Law Libraries.

The more regulations there are, the more regulations are needed – in order to update the previous regulations and (always) expand them. The only saving grace of our government should be the system of checks and balances, and transparency. It seems President Obama and Secretary Clinton have assumed the role of these two mechanisms leaving little, if any, room for US the People...

In February 1788, George Washington spoke of "two pivots" upon which the government depends. It is imperative, he said, that 1) "[the government not be] invested with more Powers than are indispensably necessary to perform the functions of a good government," and that 2) these powers be "so distributed among the Legislative, Executive and Judicial Branches that the government can never be in danger of degenerating into a monarchy or any other despotic or oppressive form, so long as there shall remain any virtue in the body of the People." Underscore: "indispensably necessary" and "degenerating into... any other despotic or oppressive form."

In other words, to paraphrase George Washington in simple modern English: 1) it is ABSOLUTELY NECESSARY that the government has only the powers necessary to perform its functions; 2) we must avoid ANY KIND OF OPPRESSIVE FORM OF GOVERNMENT by always assuring equal distribution of the governmental powers among the Legislative, Executive and Judicial Branches.

Benjamin Franklin had warned us that we shall have a "republic" only "if [we] can keep it." Today, it is the size of the government, its unbearable pressure and anonymity, lack of transparency and clear bias against the individual, which are so off-putting to every ordinary citizen who would like to vote but says: Why?

Because! We cannot demean ourselves to the bad examples of "what-does-it-matter-anyway" and "there's no there there" attitude. They maim our language, they malign us. Why is Sanders successful? He does not use these meaningless phrases and approach of ultimate indifference. What is more, he appeals – over and again – to our morals. The problem with his approach is that he does not want to show us the way or teach and protect us – he wants to command us, tell us what to do, follow HIS morals.

The only moral in democracy is: Never destroy the power of the individual! Do everything to foster individual growth and enable each one of us to exercise our constitutional rights! Ultimately, We the People have the final check on the government and its distribution of powers, which is why every vote counts. It counts in our hearts, in our minds. May no individual vanish, give away their soul to the crowd! America is the Land of the Brave, the Home of the Free – because we fight for ourselves and let no-one – not even our own government – suppress our God given rights!

We Have a Strategy

"Weakness is a friend of danger, the enemy of peace. Obama has been a weak president," Sen. Marco Rubio said. We do not have to go to Hobbes or Machiavelli for ideas on how to deal with Putin or Assad. Clearly, the latter is a puppet of the former and both swiped the floor with Obama. What is Obama's strategy? Does the Vacillator in Chief even know that, in order to execute a tactical operation with success, there must be a strategy? If not, we may win every little struggle, liberate 70 here, add 50 there, release 5 for 1 or 1 for 0 while 4 are still imprisoned in Iran... It seems to me that what the Red Liner in Chief is doing is playing fantasy football!

The White House provides the following "Four Pillars of the U.S Strategy against ISIL:"

1. A systematic campaign of airstrikes against ISIL, which begins: "Working with the Iraqi government..." proceeds to "humanitarian missions" so that "Iraqi forces go on the offense," and bravely sums up that "the President will not hesitate to take action." I do not see blowing a random truck in the desert and some vacuous warehouse elsewhere as a "systematic campaign." Every strategy is drawn on paper. Its goals must be material, time-oriented and achievable. "Working with" the enemy (someone who burns your flag and calls for your death is an enemy) and supplying "humanitarian missions" do not constitute a strategy. Obama is like a girl looking for a strong boyfriend to protect her image and make her look good in front of other girlfriends. Of course, she will not be very close with the "boyfriend" and will not tell him everything... The chief complaint President Putin expressed (in his tête-à-tête with Charlie Rose) was lack of cooperation in the area of intelligence. Putin said he would at least like to know where our interests lie and where our strikes and forces, if any, operate.

2. Increased support to forces fighting ISIL on the ground is the second point given as "strategy" by the White House. We have just sent 50 "boots" (please, call them troops or military or simply men – when a man dies, the

boots remain, a token of the dead soldier at his funeral, thus the term "boots" presumes his death – is that why you pronounce "corps" as "corpse?" Indeed, "They Died with Their Boots on…" but they were more than just "boots" before they died!

"The U.S. has sent a small contingent…" that does "not have a combat mission, but [is] providing the support needed for Iraqi forces to go on the offense," the second point of this "strategy" reveals. What does this mean? There is no offense in progress (the Iraqis have to, as yet, go into offence) and our 50 Special Forces soldiers are there to somehow "stimulate" Iraqis courage. Imagine we had sent 50 tanks to the Western Front in 1945 but ordered them to just drive around and show off in order to stimulate the courage of the French resistance. Thank God there were no weaklings where it mattered when Hitler was in power!

3. Drawing on our substantial counterterrorism capabilities to prevent ISIL attacks is proudly stated as the third point of this White House "strategy," expounding that we should be "working with our partners, we are redoubling our efforts to cut off ISIL's funding, improve our intelligence, strengthen our defenses, counter ISIL's warped ideology, and stem the flow of foreign fighters into and out of the Middle East." It is necessary to cite the whole sentence, in order to see the cringing spinelessness in context: What "partners?" Putin? Assad? We have as yet to see any military cooperation with Abdel el-Sisi or Netanyahu… Of course, it is difficult for a weak man to admit that he is weak and stand by someone stronger, self-assured, and decisive; someone who does not need flattery and mirrors of kowtowing faces to know where he stands.

"Redoubling our efforts…" – when you "redouble" zero, what do you get, Mr. O? Moreover, we are not "redoubling" airstrikes but our "efforts to cut off ISIL's funding." How? By lifting the sanctions on Iran and sending them $160bil? To "counter ISIL's warped ideology" – what does that mean? Why can we not call a terrorist a TERRORIST?! "Warped ideology" literally means "thinking twisted by heat."

I watched Fluffy Iglesias on Comedy Central the other day and he cracked a joke about his show in Saudi Arabia. They took him to a desert in the middle of nowhere (comedy is banned in public places, cities…). There, the audience was split in 2 halves by the center line (women to the right, men to the left) and the front rows of women all looked like terrorists (only a narrow chink for the eyes showing). Nonetheless, a Muslim man approached him before the show and said: "In America, you think we look sour, like dis, because we hate you," he paused. "You should be living in 120 degrees all year round," he explained. "It's the heat! Not all Arabs hate Americans – most of us look like dis," he said, warping and twisting his face, "because of the heat!"

I suppose Mr. O watched Comedy Central to pick up the language to formulate his strategy…

4. Providing humanitarian assistance to innocent civilians displaced by ISIL is the final point of this "strategy." White House says: "We cannot allow innocent communities to be driven from their homelands." Really? I suppose Mr. O watches only NBC, because both operate under the same heading: "Too Little, Too Late!"

Last time I checked on the BBC World Service, the invasion of Muslims to Europe is in full swing. Some countries take only Christians (Slovakia, Czech Republic), others negotiate quota (Hungary, Poland, Denmark…), yet others plead with Brussels to "take and distribute them" (Italy, Greece) while most refuse to take any (Spain, Finland, Hungary, Slovenia) and others are left out to hang dry (Bulgaria, Romania). Germany and Sweden are the greatest of charities – provided that they can force the others into Banki Full Moon smiles. Are there any "innocent communities" left in Syria?

Naturally, it is a part and parcel of WH "strategy" to accept 250,000 Muslim dependents before Mr. O is out of office.

Of course, there are laws, but who bothers with laws – we have – ehm – a strategy!

Rationalizing Terror?

So we call them "masterminds..." This weekend, CNN recapped two terrorist attacks which preceded Paris but were in all respects eerily similar: the Kenya Westgate Mall attack in 2013 and the twelve coordinated terror attacks in Mumbai in November 2008. Terrorists shot indiscriminately, went from a restaurant to the main railway station, machine-gunning everybody they liked. A witness survivor described them "like children with guns, deciding whom to kill." One of the terrorists survived and was subsequently questioned: "Did you feel no remorse?" He said, "Yes, but the man said 'if you want to be a big man, like me, you have to do it' – and he did it, so I did it too."

"Masterminds?" Thanks to the Indian Secret Service, we could actually hear the conversations that the terrorists had on the phone: 35 SIM cards had been sold to terrorists and 3 of them were activated during the attack. The conversation between the two "masterminds" was as follows:

"Comrade, kill the hostages. You never know when the police will attack. Kill them now!"

"Yes Comrade Superior."

"Do it now. I want to hear you do it." (Extended conversation, more delay: Comrade Inferior was making excuses why the killing of the hostages should be postponed. Eventually:)

"Yes Comrade Superior." (Two shots fired, hostages killed.)

"God is with you! Allah is great!"

"Yes Comrade Superior."

"Remember, for your mission to succeed, you must die!"

"Yes Comrade Superior."

"Leave the phone on and go and attack. I am watching it on TV. They are on the roof now. Go and attack. Do not let them take you alive!"

"Yes Comrade Superior."

The term "Comrade Superior" is a very apt translation of the term the Terrorists used. This "Comrade Superior" called the other by name, the way a school principal or class head teacher would call upon a child reading his homework. A master-servant relationship was apparent throughout the entire communication. The terrorist "on the scene" was acting as if hypnotized, a real "servant-mind." What is more, there is a deeply Freudian subtext underlying this communication, which is likewise disconcerting, in particular in view of what we have heard about how common it is in this "society" that small boys are regularly raped by grown-up ISIS members...

We speak of their "sophistication" in operating on underground computer networks and coordinating attacks as if they were Silicon Valley wizards. Whatever they do have, in terms of logistics and functional ideas, they have stolen from Western Civilization. Their mental development is that of a 10-year-old child playing a computer game and arranging a "party" with his friends via cell phone.

Indeed, how much "sophistication" does it take to take a gun from someone who virtually forces it upon you and then go and pull a trigger, thinking: "I am God! I can kill anyone I choose!"? I wonder what is worse: Obeying orders because you are "hypnotized" and psychologically abused; or because you "have to" and there is no way out; or because you like it...?! After all, the Nazi war criminals in Nurnberg also professed to have "only obeyed orders..."

A brave German journalist who spent significant time inside the "state of ISIS" recently described this "state" on CNN as a "real state" with their own police, system of administration, even schools, where children are indoctrinated into their version of Islam and taught how to fight and kill. This "state" was begun by Al Baghdadi with ex-Saddam troops and Suni renegades inside the Buka prison in Iraq. Merely stating that Al Qaida was suppressed at the end of President Bush's second term is misleading because the indoctrination, initiation, instigation and expansion of radical Islamic ideology had never been greater. The one had been suppressed militarily but it was reborn into the other.

There is a certain rationale common to all of us, to my knowledge best expressed by a French writer-philosopher and activist Jean Rostand: "Kill one man, and you are a murderer. Kill millions of men, and you are a conqueror. Kill them all, and you are a god." (Thoughts of a Biologist, 1938) This consists of a very simplistic logic, which overcomes the evil of killing by diminishing the value of the individual human being: the more people there are, the less the value of the individual.

Communist societies were based on this indirectly: the value of the individual was "equalized" to the point at which only the Party Law and Party Word (Party Committee's word led by the Dictator-Populist) mattered. People were told they were incapable of free thinking because the Party knew better and would take care of them. The situation within ISIS is eerily similar to that of a totalitarian state – only so much worse for the fact that children are taught how to kill and hate.

Rights? The only right you have is to die for Allah. What ISIS "provides" under the cloak of power and security is the illusion of greatness, the delusion of grandeur, the dream of a super-human being somewhere in the Beyond, with "full breasted maidens, grapes and wine." It appalls me that Muslims everywhere are not up in arms about the fact that the gang of 8-9 terrorists who perpetrated the recent Paris attacks had plotted their killing spree in a Belgian pub, were not even religious (breached all prohibitions Quran postulates on alcohol and drugs), were registered petty criminals with long records for theft and robbery, and the girl who was thought to have blown herself up had "converted to Islam" three months ago and likewise had a long rap sheet for drug trafficking and other crimes!

We can bomb the hell out of them – we will always win over evil and hatred – but if Muslims themselves do not step up to the plate, their religion will be destroyed. Religion of Peace? That is pure political correctness, propaganda of Obama's administration. Buddhism, Hinduism, Judaism and

Christianity are all more PEACEFUL than Islam, which is fundamentally a violent religion. It does not have to be – it is because that is how the modern-day imams interpret it and preach it in a vicious proselytizing way to their "sheep." Instead, pursuant to Quran, they should teach: piety, humility, honor, equality, brotherhood, morality and respect for elders, and even peace!

RADICAL ISLAMISTS' notion of Allah creates the ideal of super-human power to which everyone can connect and become a part of – as soon as they accomplish their suicide mission. Imagine Nietzsche on a cocktail of steroids rewriting Zarathustra! When I see those crowds blindly yelling "Allah Akbar!" I recall Hitler rallies and their "Sieg Heil!" I also recall the communist rallies I experienced in my own childhood – same thing.

These Jihad "warriors" may appear like children playing with guns but the results are much too real. What does ISIS give them? A reporter on CNN said: "None of them ever held a job, power, a girl's hand... ISIS offers them all that." They get a wife, the gun gives them power – and their job is to kill. What a power it is!

Rostand would probably suggest dropping a couple of nukes at their center positions, as there are hardly any Good People left there now. It makes little difference how you bomb them though, as long as the MYTH OF JIHAD is perpetuated. This is achieved by their propaganda. ISIS propaganda shorts are psychologically sophisticated in that they mix violence with power and faces of smiling, welcoming "comrades." All is underscored by powerful melodramatic music, which reminds me of Communist gatherings: it is the music of the mass, injecting the mass with superhuman powers. In between, you will notice an occasional warm handshake, pat on the shoulder, wink of camaraderie and friendship – apparent "love" their "recruits" are longing for. Killing is merely a means to the end. The end, paradoxically, is altogether humane.

However, this humane end defeats itself and ends in ultimate tragedy – death! Every totalitarian state leads its individual citizens to destruction: some do so under the guise of equality and better life for everybody, others under the pretense of Paradise in the Beyond. Belief in something higher, something bigger, something beyond me is what guides and motivates many of us. Belief is positive. It does not need a cause or reason. Once a reason is projected into belief, this reason may be manipulated by someone who does not believe but only wants to manipulate, rule, aggrandize and empower himself.

"Cut the Bullshit!" Says Israel's Culture Minister

Mexican President has recently compared Donald Trump to Hitler and Mussolini. This statement was initially made with respect to his "rise" but was soon stripped of all PC petals: several Harvard-weaned left-wing ideologues and other "op-ed" pundit Sanders-lovers have promptly repeated Nieto comparing Trump to Hitler without any qualms! How come no-one is upset and abhorred by this outrageous defamation which casts aspersions on our political system and our culture as much as it does on Donald Trump and millions of his followers?!

When they asked Dr. Carson how he explained to the foreign media the "despicable row" on the Republican primary stage, Dr. Carson replied that we were all appalled and felt ashamed. I am not! It is democracy at work, you foreign indoctrinated left-wing idiots! Watch and learn!

Nieto is the most corrupt Mexican politician in recent history. His mother pomaded his hair with lemon juice to make it stick and called him "Quique" when he was a boy – short for Enrique – which means: "Master of the estate." She brought him up to be a politician. He has never worked outside of politics, never held a job, knows nothing about business except the theory from his "MA in business" – probably just enough to learn how to tax and undermine small businesses. Like Sanders, Nieto has always been a socialist. He rules over a decrepit corrupt system based on three parties which vie with one another for socialist primacy.

The Institutional Revolutionary Party Nieto represents has held power in the country for 71 years, first as the National Revolutionary Party, then as the Party of the Mexican Revolution. It is a full member of the Socialist International, which is a congregation of socialist-communist parties from around the world under the Marxist heading: "Proletariat of the World, Unite!" (I vividly recall how the communists slobbered in the 1980s over Andrea Papandreu, Greek commie PM, former head of the Socialist International...) The other two significant parties in Mexico are of the same disposition: the left-wing PRD (Party of the Democratic Revolution), and National Action Party (PAN). No wonder Mexico, pobre Mejico, is so corrupt! It has been ruled by socialist for over half a century! The country is roughly comparable to the Chicago or Detroit under 30 years of Democrats' "rule" – only worse off, because there is no way out and it has been like this for generations.

Do you have a Hispanic friend? I do. Ask them what they think about Nieto. I did. I was told Nieto is the worst they have had for a long time. He married his soap opera actress of a wife to win the elections and corruption, drug trade, and the system of socialist perks have only gotten worse under him. Nieto is a nephew of the former Governor of the State of Mexico. He himself started as a notary public and soon "graduated" to the Governor of the State of Mexico... Why does no-one speak about these facts? Let me tell you why – it is not politically expedient, not something Obama-lovers would find appealing.

Today, Obama is meeting with the "good-looking Trudeau" (in Obama's words), "thawing" U.S.-Canada relations. What exactly is "thawing?" Meanwhile, he called the Middle East "situation" a state of "Cold Peace!" Cold Peace? It is impossible not to notice the "climate change" references! Let us not forget that all "Green Parties" around the world (in particular in Europe) are 100% composed of communists! It is a veneer – alas, too thin not to see through.

One cannot help comparing Trudeau, a second generation socialist (his father was Canada's Prime Minister) to Nieto. The main topics of the Obama-Trudeau gay socialist pow-wow are climate change and TPP. The latter is called "free trade" but is anything but: the socialist are transforming the words "free trade" into a commie vehicle. How? It is another thinly-disguised PC term for "down with walls and borders," a communist motto of the Second International and Socialist International: the "proletariat of the world" must "unite" against all capitalists of the world – it is the "evil capitalists" that build walls and fences to separate the proletariat of the world!

Let us summarize: Iran has fired two nuclear missiles with "Israel Must Be Wiped Out" written on them, halted talks on oil freeze, has executed one thousand people last year, including children (under 18) for drug possession and "sex crimes;" North Korea has likewise fired two short-range missiles with "miniature nuclear warheads" on them, conducted at least one nuclear test; China has usurped the South Sea international trade hub (where we sent 2 "two" bombers – to do what exactly – threaten China?) and Obama speaks about "thawing permafrost," "thawing icebergs," and "thawing relations with Canada..." Obama's brain is thawing – that is the only climate change in America!

Is anyone surprised Netanyahu turned down Obama's "invitation?" Israel's minister of culture Miri Regev said: "Cut the bullshit!" As a Moroccan-born woman, former brigadier-general in the Israel Defense Forces, she has had her share of discrimination... She would not go about whining, asking the government for more "fairness." Like Donald Trump, she approaches the issue from a pragmatic point of view, quoting the ancient Chinese philosopher of war Sun Tzu: "Cut the Bullshit!"

Brussels - a City Divided

Donald Trump has described Brussels as a "hellhole," adding that it was a beautiful city once. If so, it must have been before I lived and worked there, before the Maastricht Treaty. I worked in the very center of EU. I lived on Archimedes Street, nearby the Royal Arms Museum, and I often used the Schuman Metro station to go downtown.

Brussels has always been a City Divided – by income, race, national origin, even by weather... For all the Babel of languages there, with everyone speaking English, German, French and Flemish (even at home), no-one really feels a secure "national identity." This is clearly apparent the moment you speak with people. They will tell you "my mother is French, my father Flemish, my brother lives and works in Germany, we watch the BBC..." What language do you speak at home? "I speak French with my mom, Flemish with my dad..." Assimilation? Think again! The lack of identity, strong patriotism, national feeling, love for the country... show in the demure expression. If I did not know any better, I would say it is the diet of worms made them so – big, small, tiny frozen and fresh worms – supermarket shelves are lined with them!

Brussels is a gloomy city with very little sunshine, where days are short, skies cloudy and mood generally somber. When I first arrived in Brussels, I was stunned by the strange "architecture" which mixed medieval houses and modern glass-and-steel buildings virtually indiscriminately. Apparently, until the EU became headquartered here, there were no "cultural heritage" protection laws so people were free to pull down old buildings and construct new ones as they thought fit. The result is a strange mixture of old-and-new: you can still see a modern office block lined by medieval gothic-style decrepit houses.

Local people are averse to the EU, which they see as an imposition on their economy and lifestyle. I worked for the EU and was paid three times the average Belgian salary – and that was only my starting salary! In the gym, I spoke to the "locals" who frowned the moment they saw me: they could tell instantly I was not "one of them" and in that area, everyone who was not one of them belonged to the hated and despised EU, sponging on their taxes and economy.

Nonetheless, I did make a few friends and acquired better insight. I was warned not to go out after 5-6pm (i.e. "after dark") alone – anywhere! – for Brussels is a city of narrow streets, sharp corners and dangerous shadows, where drugs and prostitution are rampant. However, above all, the EU quarter where I lived, around Schumann and Maelbeek was swarming with strange, lanky, gypsy-looking "types" whose eyes were beady, piercing, merciless. This was twenty years ago! Oh, how blissfully little did I know then about terrorism…!

Brussels has its charms: once a year, in August, they carpet the Grand Old Place (Central Square downtown) with over a million flowers. It is some sort of a show-off competition among the local flower schools and sellers; then there is Belgian chocolate, probably the best in the world; another "attraction" is an awfully cute Mini-Europe: a Gulliver-land model city of European states where you can stroll between the Big Ben and Eiffel Tower, watch P&O ferries – all four to fourteen feet tall and long. The most famous of all these "charms" is probably the four feet tall statue of the "Pissing Boy" which dates back to the 17th century and celebrates a little boy who quenched the fire which had threatened to destroy the city in the 12th century. It is a cute legend. They dress the boy in different costumes and all Belgian people are mighty proud of him. So, after a long search, dedicated afternoon, I finally found the prophesied "Mannequin Pis" – and what a disappointment that was! Granted, the Danes have their "Little Mermaid," the English their "Peter Pan," and we - ? Well, we have the Statue of Liberty!

I call Brussels a "City Divided" because there is no unity. Everyone is a stranger there and for all the effort to unify and assimilate, the multiplicity of languages and cultures has made it into a shabby, unremarkable blob where people go on business when they must, and get out as soon as they find out what it is all about. In all respects, Brussels is the very opposite of New York and Belgium the antithesis of America.

Romney's Ugly Horns

The ugly horns of hypocrisy and egoism are hard to cover. In the 2008 primaries, Romney spent $110 million and won 11 states. $45 million was his, the rest from donors and special interests. He withdrew from the race on February 7. By the same time, Donald Trump spent $11 million (all of it his own) with approximately the same result (winning 10 states). The GOP anti-Trump spending is $220 million as of the end of February 2016.

In 2012, Romney used all available committees and PACs to raise funds. Both he and Obama spent approximately $1 billion each – unlike Donald Trump, not of their own money – on the campaign. Accused of "flip-flopping" on various issues (Obamacare, Medicaid, Dodd-Frank, Sarbanes-Oxley, etc.), he said: "I have been as consistent as a human being can be." Romney also supported preserving Guantanamo and the so-called "enhanced interrogation techniques" against terrorists. How is that different from Donald Trump's saying "I remain flexible to conduct deals?" In what respect can Romney claim higher ground here?

One thing Romney cannot "accuse" Donald Trump of is that he had a millionaire father – because they both did. Unlike Romney, however, who tried to hide his assets and look as malleable and amenable to the liberal voter as he could, Donald Trump has been proud of his father's "millions" because he knows they represent his family's work ethic and achievement. There is no room for envy in this country! If you had a father who worked hard all his life and made a lot of money – as opposed to, for example, a father who had immigrated here from a communist country, never learned proper English and washed dishes in a restaurant – well, neither should be held against you. The sickening socialist "fairness" has nothing to do with opportunity, and any arguments along the lines: "He inherited 200mil, no wonder he is better than I am..." have no place in America!

I recall exactly when I heard a similar sentence last time. It was in 1988, at the annual address of the Dean of the Olympic Sports Institute where I was "housed" for four years before the fall of communism. Castro was the idol of this Dean and his predilection long speeches lambasting the evil fat cat capitalists. It was not unusual for us to have to stand in rows for 5-6 hours listening to his haranguing. Castro used to hold speeches 16 hours long, we were told... Anyway, so this Comrade Dean spoke about Vaclav Havel, the chief "underground anti-communist instigator, a child of a capitalist fat pig who had inherited 200 million and Barrandov film studios from his father." The rationale that followed: He stole it from the proletariat and so the proletariat had rightfully reclaimed it for the people! As most of you grew up in this beautiful capitalist country, allow me to elucidate: "proletariat" means the ignorant, uneducated but well indoctrinated sheep that follow propaganda panderers such as Sanders or Clinton.

I would therefore urge even such stalwart conservatives as Senator Cruz to abstain from referring to the $200 million Donald Trump had allegedly inherited (disputed by his family members). It leads to nothing good. It creates an electoral magnetic field of evil which destroys the Soul of our Nation and pulls the electorate away from the founding principles of our Country. What is more, our country's politics have always been issue-driven, as opposed to the European parliamentary democracies, which are party-and-coalition driven. In the United States, we do not care what kind of Republican Mr. Smith is – what we care about is his ability to build, create and solve problems.

Why is Romney sticking out his ugly horns now, after three years of hibernation in San Diego? The $2.1Trillion running mate of his, Speaker Ryan, has already filed the necessary documents with the Federal Elections Commission. Meanwhile, apart from calling Donald Trump names, Romney did not endorse any candidate but urged the Republicans to vote for their respective candidates so that Rubio wins Florida, Kasich Ohio etc. – to achieve a "brokered convention" from which Romney and Ryan could re-emerge as winners. What winners would the two-time losers make, sneaking around in the grass at the last moment to try to ambush people's will?

Obama in Cuba – Why?!

Here we are - swamped by the "wonderful" news: "Obama Tours Old Havana in Pouring Rain!" the headlines scream, and: "Obama in Cuba: 'It's wonderful to be here!'" What tops it all? He is posing in front of the humongous portrait of Che Guevara – the communist mass murderer, revolutionary, who once swore on an image of the then recently deceased Joseph Stalin: "not to rest until the capitalist octopuses have been vanquished!"

The larger-than-life portrait of this communist animal's head in the background reminds me of the past. In 1987, I visited Romania under Ceausescu. At the time, I lived in communist Czechoslovakia and we were only allowed to travel into other communist countries. As a rule, the further east you went, the poorer and more communist-ravaged the land and population. I saw similar huge portraits of the Romanian dictator on walls and buildings. Streets were literally lined with them: Big Brother everywhere! Four years later, they would all be torn down and destroyed – and the Great Dictator also killed, Mussolini style, but 1987 was still marked as the Dark Ages of Communism.

At that time, Romania was as poor as it gets: naked children lined the train coming from "the west" begging for anything we could spare, hungrily reaching out, gathering candies from the ground. A trip east for us was the trip to our own future then... At night, the train was invaded by hordes of thieves and whatever was not securely attached was stolen. I recall the person sleeping on the bunk above me had her trunk picked from under her head and pulled out of the window as she was lying there, not even asleep – all of a sudden, the window slid open and someone pulled the trunk out. It happened in a matter of seconds!

We passed through Constanta and arrived at the Black sea. It was dark and lifeless, just like the country it shored. A man on the shore was selling small fish which resembled mackerel. Eagerly, we purchased two, looking forward to a somewhat "oriental" feast, for we were "Drylanders" from Central Europe, not bordered by any sea. The fish were salt-soaked, weeks old, dried up in the sun and completely inedible. What else do they have to eat? we wondered, venturing to a local "supermarket."

There were shelves with three things on display: Vodka, beans, and toilet paper – no milk, meat, yoghurt... nothing at all, not even bread! Later, we were told that milk and bread was available only to the locals, to be purchased at special allotment of meal tickets. Only pregnant mothers received more milk tickets, perhaps even once a week, the rest once a month, depending on the number of children in the family...

However, what surprised me the most was the absolute lack of complaints. People looked haggard, depressed, but tough. When you spoke to them, they rejoined in proud communist gestures. We had a carton of powdered milk we did not use by the time we were leaving so we decided to exchange it for a souvenir. I do not recall want knick-knack bric-a-brac it was, a pleated basket, a folklore napkin, perhaps... All I can recall is a lanky old man staring straight back at me with spite in his eyes saying in broken German he did not want my milk. I asked why. He went back behind a drape and returned with a can of beans in one hand and a framed portrait of Ceausescu in the other. "I have this - and this!" he said, flashing a row of teeth decayed by years of socialist healthcare.

If Obama was not Obama but an ordinary person going to Cuba on a vacation, there is no doubt in my mind that is what he would have experienced. Yesterday, I listened to interviews with Cuban people on CCTV: a teacher extolled the virtues of socialist education, women's equality, how Cuban literacy rates exceed those in the U.S. (?) etc.; then there was a restaurant owner proudly displaying the U.S. flag, albeit only in the last few days and inside, he said, he had a portrait of Obama side by Castro on the wall! A local professor of political science was interviewed: "Not since 1928 has there been a presidential visit. Capitalist interventions have prevented it." Finally, a teacher of English, with a suspiciously perfect native

American accent went on to emphasize how much "Americans" have yet to learn from Cuba...

Naturally, what the reporter failed to mention was that all the people interviewed had been either carefully selected and approved by the apparatchiks of the local Politburo or simply indoctrinated socialists afraid for their Party Card and cozy position in "the system." Yes, it is all about "the system" – not the individual! I recalled the eyes of the haggard old man holding the picture of Ceausescu and a can of beans...

Watching these "interviews," one can only marvel at complete absence of any criticism! To me, however, it is self-explanatory, although it cannot quite be explained in words: ideology beats reason. Criticism is what makes US better – individually and as a society. Criticism and dialogue is what undermines every totalitarian system at any stage of development, what reveals corruption, discloses deficiencies.

Here, in the United States, we believe in Pragmatism, tempered by meliorism. Pragmatism says that the effects caused by an object define that object. In other words, our concepts are not ideas but effects. Meliorism says that we cannot achieve perfection in anything but this should not detract from our trying constantly to improve. We also believe in work ethics, especially those tied to Protestantism: a healthy individual is the source a healthy society – healthy in the mind and in the body. We cannot achieve greatness by stealing or ravaging.

I grew up in communism – to criticize the system was the most grievous of transgressions. Murderers used to receive less "time" than "political rebels." We have all heard of the American student sentenced to 15 years of hard labor for allegedly stealing some advertising plaque. Imagine if he had actually smuggled in George Orwell's Animal Farm or 1984 and wanted to distribute it in some unofficial manner!

Do you recall what the motto of the Colonists was around the time of the Townsend Acts, in particular the Stamp Act and the Tea Act? To remain silent in face of such exploitation was deemed un-American and treasonous!

Those who sat at home in silence were "not real Americans" but traitors complicit in the evils of the Crown! No Taxation without Representation meant that "no private property" could be taken "without the consent of the owner!" Paradoxically, this motto was founded on the strict property laws of Great Britain. Imagine someone taking a picture with the portrait of King George and having it published in Ben Franklin's paper!

"Silence means slavery!" Sam Adams would say. That is what socialists-cum-communists want US to be: silently complicit, slaves to the system, nodding to them with a portrait of Obama or Sanders in one hand and a can of beans in the other, smiling our toothless Obamacare smile at the "hyphenated-American" reporter asking us with a heavy accent how we like it...

Well, we don't – and we won't! We are the Land of Doers, not empty-headed "dreamers" and organized disrupters who want to silence US!

No Existential Threat

"ISIS does not produce anything (therefore) poses no existential threat to US," said President Obama on the occasion of his "tango" conference in Argentina. The logic of this statement escapes me: Hitler did not produce anything; Napoleon did not produce anything... It is precisely the opposite, which is the case here: those who do not produce but destroy pose an existential threat to the rest of us.

However, this statement is more insightful into the mind of this limp-handed egoist than it appears. First of all, it shows Obama's psychology, which is firmly rooted in his notion of invincibility: he is the most powerful man in the world, guarded by the most sophisticated secret service. He is safe and no-one can harm him and his family. His primary concern has always been for himself and his "legacy."

Whenever I see Obama, I recall Norman Mailer's essay entitled the "White Negro" and Christopher Lasch's book "The Culture of Narcissism." Of course, Obama's politics are founded on Wilsonian peace-making and nation-building – antithetical to Alfred Thayer Mahan's concept of the naval power, all types of "Rough Riders" and thus also our military values and the values on which the world operates, which is to say values firmly grounded in the doctrine of the balances of powers, alliances and Machiavellian pragmatism.

Obama proclaims himself to be a pragmatist but is anything but: his concern cannot be in what works because to have such a concern in the first place, one must have an aim in mind, e.g. defeating ISIS, creating a workable relationship with Israel and Great Britain, advancing the changing purposes of the North Atlantic Alliance, etc.

Obama's "existentialist" statement underscores both his psychology and his philosophy. Psychologically, he always takes the route of least resistance, hoping to make friends with everybody. That is his primary weakness – he wants to be liked and admired, cannot accept criticism. Therefore, his philosophy is tantamount to resignation. This resignation is coupled with internal contentment, security derived from the pathology of negation: I must be weak in order to be strong; everyone who threatens me is weaker and acts out of weakness; I must remain cool at all times...

In the background, I hear the communist mottoes from Orwell's 1984: "War is Peace! Freedom is Slavery! Ignorance is Strength!" Philosophically, they can be defined as "Absurdism" and "Nihilism." They are children of existentialism. Take, for example, the completely apathetic Meursault, the main character in Camus' "Stranger." This man does not cry at his mother's funeral and when he is sentenced to death, he thinks it is somehow a natural course of life – to be punished. This Kafkaesque turning into a bug that watches others come and go, pass by, unable to do anything about life, because "being" simply "is," is at the core of Obama's life philosophy.

Norman Mailer, the author of the great war novel "The Naked and the Dead" (of which every American should have read at least the first 80 pages), describes this psychopathology in his "White Negro." This term refers to all people who are in some way products of existentialism, which started with Nietzsche's "God is dead" and completed full circle in Sartre's "existence precedes essence." Existence comes first and essence is defined by constant negation: we become something only to "unbecome" and turn into something else. A hipster-existentialist (i.e. "the white negro") avoids neurosis not by psychoanalysis and value-orientation, but by creating a workable psychopathy, which tells him to "let it be."

Likewise, Clinton's "What difference does it make at this point anyway?" is a statement profound in its shallowness: nothing really matters at the end of the day. It is a statement made by Camus' main character – rather than being Kafka's bug, upside down, kicking one's tiny legs in the air, unable to communicate, cry for help – she develops a workable psychopathy of nihilism.

It is this psychopathy which is the mangled version of pragmatism: we avoid danger to our existence by letting our essence take whatever form the world desires it to take.

Our Constitution, our Bill of Rights, written laws, history – they form a stable, immutable essence. This essence must be erased in order to preserve our existence. At the same time, self-preservation is of little concern (to Obama) because even that is only a form of transformation: if the United States should be transformed into a United Caliphate, it would make no difference to the existence of its people – such is Obama's opinion and philosophy.

Obama's "doing the wave" in the stadium, his "tango," his walking through the streets of rainy Havana... those are all symptomatic of this existential psychopathy, whose main and sole purpose is to be cool, hip, admired, and let everything else "slide." When Norman Mailer was asked: "What is existentialism?" he replied: "It's sort of playing everything by the ear." No doubt, Kierkegaard and even Nietzsche and Sartre would agree.

After all, when "God is dead," everything is allowed. To ask about Obama's religion is like asking a bug what time it is. Religion, with all its powerful symbols, are like the symbols of statehood to him: the Statue of Liberty does not symbolize national strength, power looking to the rising sun; but, rather, it stands for a mangled version of Lazarus and tango, defined by connoisseurs as "vertical solitude." Taken to the ultimate logical conclusion, Obama's resignation is no different than the approach of the suicide bomber, who welcomes death as the ultimate equalizer and liberator – except, in Obama's case, it is the death of the essence of what it means to be an American (albeit mere existence shall be continued).

NATO and Obama's "Cold Peace"

When President Obama speaks of the Middle East as being in a state of "Cold Peace," he is being delusional. Even as we speak, people are actually dying as a result of his incompetence and weakness. The man who entered the White House as a man of peace and reconciliation has caused more suffering and death in the world than we have seen since Vietnam. What is more, his "peace-making" is founded on social engineering and making our army weak. More aircraft, ships, helicopters... have been decommissioned during Obama's "reign" than during the terms of any of his predecessors since World War II. The number of our troops is at all time low. In fact, never since the end of World War II have we had so few troops!

Obama simply wants to keep his eyes closed to "see no evil," much like a peacock sticking his head into a heap of sand. Meanwhile, Iran has been working hard to develop long range missiles and nuclear weapons, NORAD's intercepts of Russian nuclear bombers are occurring with uncanny regularity, and Obama's "red buttons" and lines in the sand mean less to the world than those of a child playing in a sandpit. Last September, China sent five warships into Alaskan waters while Obama was visiting Anchorage, speaking about "increasing and real danger to the world" – as a result of melting glaciers!

In Europe, Obama withdrew all tanks from our bases in Germany and severely cut our presence. His first step in the "Russian reset" (as Obama's then Secretary of State Clinton termed it) was to abolish the first stage of our nuclear defense system in Poland and the Czech Republic. General Flynn stated that he has been "baffled" by his Commander-in-Chief's actions. If anyone has the power to destroy the United States, it is Russia. Instead of leading, Obama is being led by the nose – and we have to follow him.

When Donald Trump opined about the futility of NATO and our engagements abroad, Obama responded that "Trump knows nothing about how the world works."

Really? If NATO had been under proper leadership, there would have been no Muslim invasion of Europe, Ukraine would not be under Russian threat today, Libya would not be flooded by radical Islamic thugs, and Iraq would have been a growing industrial western economy.

While NATO was founded in 1949 as a response to the threat posed by the Soviet Union, its function has always been global and as much economic as military, because the two are inseparable. It was under the leadership of the United States and with the aid provided through the US-funded Marshall Plan and other means that Europe was slowly stabilized after World War II. NATO's Treaty Article 2 provides for non-military cooperation, and this article precedes all articles on military cooperation.

In turn, when Soviet Union integrated its satellites into Warsaw Pact in 1954, after West Germany joined NATO, this move was likewise made under the heading of economic cooperation within ComEcon (Council for Mutual Economic Cooperation) – a communist-directed international "market." Today, thanks to Obama's Iranian "deal," China, Russia, and Iran, all ruled by totalitarian despots, are growing economically closer than ever before. It would not surprise anyone if they formed an Eastern Cooperation Union (or some such Leviathan) to the exclusion of all western democracies.

When Donald Trump criticizes NATO as "defunct" and non-functioning, he approaches the issue from a businessman's point of view: if allies cannot provide for common defense, how can they provide for common trade? Interestingly, each time there was an actual threat, not only military but also economic cooperation among the allies increased: when the Russians touted their atomic bomb in 1949, after the outbreak of the Korean War in 1950, when Warsaw Pact forces invaded Hungary in 1956, with the Blockade of West Berlin and the construction of the wall in 1961, and even the suppression of the Spring of 1968 in Czechoslovakia – all these events brought the allies closer militarily as well as economically.

Indeed, European Union would have been impossible without NATO – and without American leadership! The events leading to the current EU all either closely precede or follow and trail the allies' military challenges listed above: the Hague Conference (1948), founding of the European Coal and Steel Community (1952), European Economic Community (1957), Euratom (treaty on nuclear & atomic cooperation, 1958), the Merger Treaty (establishing "European Communities" in 1967), and the Maastricht Treaty in 1992 (foreseeing unification of the former communist bloc countries) have all been results of military crises and resulting cohesion of powers. It does not take a Kissinger to see that recent attacks on Brussels' airport and subway at EU headquarters constitute an assault on EU as much as against NATO, which is often perceived as the capitalist threat in the Middle East and in all other countries ruled by dictators.

During the early 1960s, NATO adopted the strategic doctrine of "Massive Retaliation" if the Soviet Union attacked any of the Allied Powers – NATO would respond with nuclear weapons. This was the famous Doctrine of Deterrence, based on power, not words. Cold War, a standoff - sort of "separate but equal" peace - was only possible because Soviet Union and the United States posed mutually commensurate weight on the balances of powers – not because there would have been some magic "deal" on mutual "peaceful development" of nuclear energy, as modern socialists (including President Obama) envision.

However, this is impossible under what Donald Trump correctly characterized as an "obsolete" and "largely defunct" NATO. The new NATO must be focused on the problem of the Middle East, which endangers all NATO allies today. Warsaw Pact had been dissolved under Vaclav Havel's auspices in 1991. NATO has continued to exist on the premise of some extant danger. Meanwhile, all European countries have been infiltrated by subversive Islamists, and the virus of socialism and communism has continued to infiltrate all free-minded peoples, much like cancer vanquished in one organ moves to another.

We know what Obama has done – nothing. We know what Clinton would do – another cackle of a "reset" with anyone, just to take a picture and be praised. For what? More of our brave men would fall prey to marauding Muslim hordes and failed promises... We need a strong president who will lead the NATO allies to victory, which means out of this absurd communist miasma of "cold peace" – bearing in mind that it is as much a business venture as a military one.

Donald Trump is correct that NATO has failed repeatedly – on a large scale, it failed in Libya and it failed to prevent the Muslim invasion of Europe. Undermined security means eroded business cooperation.

Donald Trump is incorrect that NATO has no purpose and should perhaps be abolished. It would be exceedingly difficult to set up a similar organization today, based on common defense against the guerilla tactics of the Islamists. Under American leadership, NATO can take action: renew and boost business cooperation, which will lead to military cooperation. Our trade agreements should be focused on our NATO allies, not on perfunctory on countries that neither want to be helped nor deserve our help. It does not matter how we regain unity – but someone must be at the helm, not playing golf and dancing tango!

Obama's Winning Friends Is Making Enemies

Obama's policy of winning friends has turned our friends into enemies. When he abolished the missile defense systems in Poland and the Czech Republic, the argument was that Iran did not have the capability to manufacture and use long-range nuclear missiles. Even then, upon Obama's first election, this argument was false, because Iran had possessed and successfully tested the solid-fuel Sejil missile in May 2009, which had an estimated range of 1,560 miles, thus was capable of reaching Prague and Warsaw with a one-ton payload. The International Atomic Energy Agency said in 2009 that Iran had "sufficient information" to build an atomic bomb and was able to "overcome problems" involved in its delivery system. We can only surmise and assume that 8 years into Obama's misadministration of foreign policy, situation is even worse for US, for NATO, and for all of our former friends.

There is no doubt in my mind that recent Russian aggression in the Baltic Sea is a direct outcome of Obama's policy of conciliation and "flexibility" toward Russia. Yesterday (mid-April 2016), Polish defense minister stated that Russia's "systematic acts of aggression" indicate that it "will not stop with Ukraine." This is a very serious allegation, in particular in view of the Crimean crisis.

Earlier this month, two Russian warplanes flew simulated attack passes near a U.S. guided missile destroyer which had just left the Polish port of Gdynia. A U.S. official said this was one of the most aggressive encounters in recent history. Yet, nothing happened. Kerry issued a few gestures indicating disapprobation. Those are empty gestures, and Putin knows it, because there is no "club" of nuclear missile defense in his hand. What is more, NATO and Europe is too preoccupied with the Muslim Invasion and crisis produced by the liberal complacency of PC-ridden politics – and lack of American leadership within NATO.

It is not coincidental that these attacks (such as the 11 "fly-bys" on destroyer Cook, followed by helicopter intimidation) occur predominantly in the Baltic Sea – close to Latvia, Lithuania and Estonia, former Russian republics which Putin eyes as cherries on the cake of Russian re-unification. These republics were among the first of EU "associated countries." In culture, they are as European as Poland and the Czech Republic. In economy, they are among the richest in Europe.

Estonia boasts large oil reserves, stores of uranium, granite, rare earths and oxides. Lithuania has extensive plastic polymer industry and other plants, including top-notch IT technology and telecommunication firms. With corporate tax rate of 15% (5% for small companies), Lithuania is also extremely attractive to foreign firms and one may encounter may English, Italian, and even American firms have their IT centers here. Technology and economy closely connects these "Baltic republics" to Poland, Sweden and Finland. They have common internet, naval routes, and are interdependent in trade. All three are now also members of NATO and attacking them would mean attacking NATO.

Last year, a Swedish passenger aircraft had a narrow miss with a Russian surveillance plane. In December, NATO described Russian "passes" as a threat to regional civil aviation. We all remember the shooting down of Malaysian Airlines Flight over Ukraine in 2014. These incidents have only been increased as Obama's administration entered its final year. Is the leeway and blasé attitude President Obama shows vis-à-vis Russian aggression the example of his "flexibility" – so infamously predicted during his 2012 meeting with Putin?

Clinton's Corruption and Sanders' Communism

Today, having won the Cold War, Balkans, Iran... capitalism has made us too complacent and unaware of what the treat of communism really means. For Clinton and Sanders alike, everything that is wrong with our society is the fault of the "system:" there is "systemic racism," "systemic incarceration" of black people, "systemic" police violence, etc. Clinton's e-mail scandal is a product of systemic hatred and a right-wing conspiracy. This "systemic suspicion" falls on anyone who is not part of the progressive movement: Why not? They must have some secret funds in an offshore account! They must be part of a larger conspiracy! "They" are not "us!"

This "us against them" is the old Marxist motto: "If you are not with us, you are against us!" Lenin, Stalin, Hitler, Brezhnev, Khrushchev and others used to say. Clinton's tepid "Trumpian" take-off "Make America Whole again" means "It's us against them" – the socialist worker against the capitalist "pig" or, as Sanders says, "the not-haves against the haves." Property envy is a fundamental building stone of socialism. Socialism is not about striving harder to be better but about destroying what the other one has in order to be equally poor. Here is a joke which used to be traded among the youth when I was growing up in socialism:

"In Germany, when your neighbor buys a sports car, you work harder so that you can buy one too. In America, you work even harder so that you buy a better one. In Russia, you wait till dark and then venture out with a sharp key to scratch the beautiful shiny metal finish on that damned car you can't afford..."

It is not a joke, it is a way of thinking – the socialist way.

Not many people know that Hillary Clinton knew Mr. Alinsky even better than Bernard Sanders did, although the latter has more in common with him personally, being of similar orthodox Jewish dissent, revolting primarily against his parents and their idiosyncratic doctrine of Jewish allegiance. Clinton spent a whole year seeing Alinsky on a weekly basis. He taught her the fundamentals of community organizing and "establishment baiting" (in Alinsky's words). In turn, she dedicated a much praised 100-page thesis on his theory of community organizing entitled "There Is Only the Fight" which, frankly, sounds very much like Hitler's "My Fight..." (Mein Kampf).

That is the problem with revolutionaries: they each feel they are great individuals singled out for slaughter. This is not a doom but a blessing to them: they want to be martyrs or, rather, they need to be seen as martyrs by others. Alinsky's motto is as follows: bait the establishment, provoke them, and the moment you are attacked, stand up and say you fight for the people! Hitler rose to power in the same fashion. If anyone should dare oppose you, deny the accusations and attack them on your turf!

Hillary Clinton has met her match in Bernard Sanders though, who practiced what Alinsky preached even as she was learning the ropes as Alinsky's favorite pupil. Obama and Sanders, both active Chicago community organizers, have been on par ideologically from the very start. Hillary Clinton descended to their level of thinking about people and society only upon thorough analysis and as a result of personal disappointment.

As apparent from her autobiography, Clinton prides herself on being "of the people." Of Welsh descent, daughter of coalminers' on her father's side, and Canadian emigres from Bristol on her mother's side, Hillary Rodham was raised in a conservative household and her first political escapades were on the Republican side. At the age of thirteen, while most of us were occupied doing homework, playing sports or plotting a date, Hillary Rodham was on the streets of Chicago helping canvass for the 1960 U.S. presidential election. Having "detected fraud" in Richard Nixon's campaign, she turned to Goldwater as a volunteer.

While Sanders has always been an aspiring communist, revolting against his parents' religious orthodoxy, Hillary Clinton's socialism is tepid and moderate. Clearly, a la Bill, she is planning to run on a more middle-of-the-road platform in the general election. Hillary Rodham began to lean to the left during the Civil Rights Movement and the Vietnam War. Her mindset has never been 100% socialist and I doubt she even knows what the word really means. When Sanders is attacking her "qualifications" because she is supported by Wall Street and the "big money," he is doing so from the position of a left-wing communist whose ideology does not permit capitalism at all.

What Sanders fails to see is that corruption is not a systemic failure but stems from the integrity of the individual. The political system either upholds it and holds individuals accountable, as capitalism with its system of checks-and-balances and free speech does, or covers it – as socialism with its conformity and subjugation shall mandate. Now, with the shadow of the Panama Papers hanging over her head, Clinton has swiftly raised doubts whether Senator Sanders is "qualified to be president." The press instantly focused on this issue, rather than covering the link between Clinton's campaign manager Podesta and Sberbank, infamous lynchpin in the Panama Papers.

What the latter yields remains to be seen. However, as to the question Mme. Clinton raised: Sanders is a totalitarian bureaucrat with no experience in the real world; Clinton is a failed Secretary of State whose only qualification is that she lost to a novice Senator in the previous race and he made her his own mercenary minion out of pity and shame. What makes Trump and Cruz popular is their unapologetic American Pride and self-reliance, qualities on which this country was built and which we so sorely need and lack in our public representatives today.

The threat of communism is the threat of ignorance and weakness. The threat of communism is the threat of dependency and desperation. The threat of communism is the threat of family disintegration. Ever since Plato, communists have been fond of abstractions and concepts such as "I am a citizen of the world" and "the state is your family" and "a philosopher is the best king…" The reason why the young are inspired by communism is because they want to make the world better. Alas, they know not how the world works – that making yourself better, furthering yourself through hard work and self-reliance is the only way to make the world a better place. Sanders has never learned it. Clinton knows it but she is too corrupt to mind – she would do anything to "equal" her husband...

Highest hopes and aspirations end in sadness and desperation when one believes his or her own propaganda. America is about idealism and the image of the Self, yes. True Americans – why, we are Walt Whitmans – all of us! Alas, at the same time, we know that our forefathers died for the liberties we enjoy, and that our compassion and empathy is the result the Civil War, and many other wars, and that no "Ism" comes to us as a Savior. We shall never be subdued. We shall never fall prey to an ideology. The only qualification our President must have is our Trust – and his Faith in US.

Gray Mouse of Socialism

Gray people living in gray houses having gray lives and gray destinations... Socialism is based on mediocrity. Anyone who excels, anyone with aspirations and individuality, anyone who dares challenge the order and demonstrates ability – is not welcome. Left-forward, march! Sing the International and be happy in the herd!

You can see this still, anywhere socialism is extant: China, for instance. Chinese students coming to the United States are devoid of imagination. They excel in math and memorization, but give them an essay topic – and they are like a stranded seaman on a raft without a paddle or sail. They sail with the wind.

Socialism is founded on conformity. It subjugates character and individuality, shaves off sharp edges and disciplines you whenever you diverge, refusing to toe the line. When I was in kindergarten, they used to take us out for a walk. We had a rope with regular knots on it and we had to hold the rope, arranged in pairs like little soldiers. We were not allowed to run or scatter. In high school, we all had military drill exercises in PE classes: turns, salutes, or simply standing in line – all in regular, precise order.

Perhaps that is what is needed when people do not appreciate their freedom? Perhaps, there is too much liberty in our modern capitalist world and people do not appreciate it? Perhaps, we all long for order and want to be drilled and commanded?

Our Founding Fathers gave US a Republic: the response is attributed to Ben Franklin at the close of the Constitutional Convention of 1787, when queried as he left Independence Hall on the final day of deliberation. Dr. James McHenry's notes read: "A lady asked Dr. Franklin: 'Well Doctor what have we got a republic or a monarchy.' – 'A republic,' replied the Doctor 'if you can keep it.'"

Indeed – our Freedom, if we can keep it!

The magnitude of Sanders' supporters is truly astounding. They will argue that capitalism is evil – or at least so imperfect that we need socialism, or "more socialism." They are persuaded that "we already have socialism" and point at the social security and Medicare as examples. Those government instituted redistribution plans have nothing to do with socialism though. They could not exist in socialism, because socialism takes from everyone and allots everyone the same: there is one plan for everybody. It is inconceivable to sue and get paid when injured, because government is the only insurer and you cannot sue the socialist government.

Plans like Medicare and social security are the advantages of market economy: hospitals and insurance companies still compete, although under the umbrella of state & federal governments. Some regulation is good, but not when it concerns the outcome or distribution. You can regulate where the crash barriers are, where the sidelines will be and where the goalposts are. You cannot regulate everything along one white line pole-to-pole – not unless you want to turn the whole state into a prison.

Imprisoned minds, imprisoned bodies. Socialists do not build walls to keep people out – but to keep them in. As someone who was arrested crossing the border to the Free World, strip-searched, cross-interrogated while machine guns were pointed at me in cross-lights of two lamps in an underground bunker by two KGB super-rats, subsequently jailed and publicly reprimanded, I have stories to tell...

To those who want more socialism, I would say: there is no perfect system or political arrangement. The best system is such which provides for most freedom, competition, self-determination and self-reliance. It is not socialism in any of its forms. Liberal democracy is not socialism. Democratic socialism is socialism. Social democracy is a term misapplied to liberal democracy by Sanders and other fanatics who want to mislead you. Social democracy is "social" only to the extent to which it is "liberal" and representative. Representative democracy may be called social democracy, but never democratic socialism. The latter is an oxymoron, because there is nothing democratic about socialism. Socialism is a system of government redistribution of everything: from your personal property to how much you are allowed to learn, to your healthcare.

Recently, I have been scornfully asked by a "Bernie" supporter who accidentally crossed my path: "What do you base it on? Yourself? Ha-ha!" Well, yes, my experience. What more do you want than the experience of someone who knows, who has been there? If you will not read the Animal Farm, 1984, Hayek and others... at least, pray to God, listen to someone who means well and knows better.

Socialism starts by instructing you what to say and when. You may not say anything against the Party. The next step is to make everybody belong to the Party, to "turn them." Most will do it out of "free will," because it will provide them with a more secure job, a position in a government agency or organization which depends on the system. Next, all opposition must be ridiculed and restricted, forced onto the Right Path. If they resist, they will suffer under the pressure of government Agencies: properties over $1mil must belong to the State or some larger cooperative under the state, taxes on everything which endangers the Party, for instance guns, corporate mergers, foreign imports which undermine "domestic" companies (those in close cahoots with the Party). You see, underground economy, bribes and corruption will be all that is left from free market under socialism...

The greatest paradox is that people will follow the idealist panderer to the grave – and beyond – with hope and trust that they are doing it to better humankind and make everyone better off, somehow more equal and fair and just... They call it "social justice," but it is, in fact, "socialist justice." In capitalism, people give freely for charitable causes which the market (market is people) determines worthy of support. In socialism, government gives equally to all causes it deems politically expedient. In capitalism, you may achieve true greatness, which is reflected by the appreciation of other people in your income and living standard. In socialism, only the Party is great; individuals have the same "equal" "social" value, thus they all deserve the same and will be allotted the same.

When Sanders calls for taxing Wall Street and that "Wall Street" will pay for everything – and his supporters blindly repeat it – they do not pause to think: What is Wall Street? A street? A corporation? What is it? Wall Street is a figure of speech, which refers to all US financial markets, similar to when we say Hollywood and we refer to the film industry. When Sanders says "Wall Street will pay for your college," he is saying "U.S. financial markets will pay." This means the free market economy will be taxed – every transaction on every good, every stock purchase or sale. Your parents and family who own stocks will own nothing, because it will all be "used by the government." The goods will have to be more expensive because all companies will be taxed not twice (currently 40%) but three times: the government will determine the "final tax" or "value added tax" – the value? You may get something in the end, if you still want to go to college. But why would you, if everyone is paid the same and your job is secured – because everything is in some way tied to the Party and the Government...? Go back to your gray house and be happy in your gray existence, you, gray mouse of socialism!

I am not making this up. I have been there before – and I ain't going back!!!

Clinton's Corrupt Camp and the Panama Papers

The infamous 11.5 million documents, summarily referred to as the "Panama Papers," have become known as the "biggest financial leak in history," exceeding even the Wiki Leaks. Technically, these documents are subject to attorney-client privilege, because they are held by the Mossack Fonseca Law Firm. How the documents were compromised remains a mystery. Allegedly, a person known only as John Doe sent these documents as a file to the Munich newspaper Süddeutsche Zeitung, a struggling paper which has been under water for over ten years.

In spite of the ominous "Wait what's coming yet!" given by the paper as a response to the question "How come there are no Americans involved?" – at first sight, it is perhaps unlikely that but a handful of less important public figures would be involved in this scandal. The International Consortium of Investigative Journalists ("ICIJ") continues to sieve through the files, but in view of the fact that the United States of America and Panama signed the Panama Free Trade Agreement in 2012, a bombshell remains unlikely – or so they say.

The US-Panama FTA includes provisions requiring disclosure and release of information regarding all "ownership of companies, partnerships, trusts, foundations, and other persons" to the US regulatory authorities. "If Panama had ever been an attractive destination for American offshore storage of funds, this agreement shut the door on that possibility," as John Cassidy wrote in The New Yorker.

Nonetheless, there is over 1000 US incorporation papers lodged with Mossack Fonseca which are now compromised and part of the Panama Papers. It must be noted that the scheme involving money laundering and tax evasion is based on confusion about whom the properties belong to, not their existence. Thus, a person may found a corporation plus a trust and set up an offshore account as an entity doing business elsewhere. The extent, scope and diligence with which US authorities would normally follow up

206

on such "scoundrels and scammers" (to paraphrase the notorious NBC series) pursuant to the US-Panama FTA is questionable – which means we can, indeed, expect some surprises.

For instance, it has been revealed that Russia's biggest financial institution, Sberbank, uses The Podesta Group as its lobbyist in Washington, D.C. Its CEO is Tony Podesta, who founded the Group in 1998 with his brother John, formerly chief of staff to President Bill Clinton, then counselor to President Barack Obama. Mr. Podesta is the epitome of a Democratic insider. Three Podesta Group staffers are all key "rainmakers" in Hillary Clinton's campaign: Tony Podesta, Stephen Rademaker, and David Adams. What is more, John Podesta, Tony's brother, is the chairman of that campaign, the chief architect of her plans to take the White House this November.

Russian "savings bank" Sberbank hired the Podesta Group to help its public image, which had been tainted by corruption and previous scandals, and asked them to assist in relieving them from the sanctions placed on Russia in the aftermath of the Kremlin's aggression against Ukraine. It appears that the Podestas took Sberbank's money and "laundered" it via their Panama accounts. This was naïve, to say the least, because of Sberbank's already tainted reputation and the likelihood of a U.S. probe into Mossack Fonseca. Obviously, the "climate" of "what difference does it make" and being "above the law" rains supreme in Hillary Clinton's camp.

We also know full well that the rise of socialists like Sanders here or Jeremy Corbin in Britain is also fueled by offshore-chiseled funds. In particular, Mr. Soros, who had set up his first offshore fund in the 1960s, is a true master of these schemes, which are fueled by totalitarian regimes with lack of accountability. Places like Russia, China, Saudi Arabia occur multiple times in the Panama Papers. While the Prime Minister of Iceland was forced to resign when it was revealed that he had sold a company to his wife for $1 (to avoid taxes), in totalitarian states, such accountability remains to be desired: who will depose the President of

China (heavily involved in Panama money laundering) or the members of the Syrian regime (such as the cousin of Bashar Al Assad, often described as "poster boy of corruption")?

OECD (Organisation for Economic Cooperation and Development) has attempted to deal with the problem in its "Model Tax Convention and Transfer Pricing Guidelines," which contain 1600 pages of suggestions summarily termed the "BEPS process." This "Basic Erosion and Profit Shifting" plan is to cover taxation cracks (corporations avoiding double taxation), taxes escaping from the countries where they should be accrued (individuals making money here, sending them abroad; multinational companies doing the same on larger scale) and other illicit schemes. Whether such ambitious comprehensive measures can be implemented globally – when even our own presidential candidate seems beyond legal reproach or probe – is questionable.

Trump University

Trump University was incorporated in 2004. It was launched as an educational institution in 2005. Donald Trump advertised that he could "turn anyone into a successful real estate investor." It had three tracks, gold, silver, and introductory.

The lawsuit against Trump University (and Donald Trump, also named as an individual in the complaint) was filed in August 2008. The plaintiff, Tarla Makaeff, attended Trump University's three-day "Fast Track to Foreclosure Workshop" for $1,495. One of her chief complaints was that the song "Money, Money, Money" from the Apprentice show was used to "thrill people about money" and "up-sell" them to the gold program for $34,995. Apparently "thrilled," Makaeff paid $34,995 to enroll in the Gold Elite Program, which entitled her to four three-day "advanced training workshops," a three-day "mentoring session in the field," and "training publications, software, and other materials."

In April 2009, after completing five more programs and workshops, and after seven months of the Gold Elite Program, she wrote an email to Trump University complaining that she could not pay the required tuition and thought that she did not receive the value she expected "for such a large expenditure." In response to Makaeff's email, Trump University offered more free "mentoring services" to her, which Makaeff accepted.

Having accepted these services and used them up, Makaeff then wrote to her bank as well as the Better Business Bureau, contacted government agencies, and posted on Internet message boards rants about her dispute with Trump University. Makaeff requested a refund of $5,100 from her bank for services charged for Trump University programs (had Trump refunded her this money in 2009, there would most likely have never been this lawsuit at all). In the letter to the Better Business Bureau, Makaeff requested a refund of her payments for services that she did not receive and complained of the following: "fraudulent business practices," "illegal predatory high pressure closing tactics," "brainwashing scheme[s]," "outright fraud," "grand larceny," "identity theft," "unsolicited taking of personal credit and trickery into [sic] opening credit cards," "fraudulent business practices utilized for illegal material gain," "felonious teachings," "neurolinguistic programming and high pressure sales tactics based on the psychology of scarcity," "unethical tactics," "a gargantuan amount of misleading, fraudulent, and predatory behavior," and business practices that are "criminal" etc. Some of these claims sound preposterous, especially in view of the fact that "high pressure sales tactics based on the psychology of scarcity" and "neurolinguistics programming" constitute the grounds of real estate dealing...

She published these claims on the internet, thus Trump University countersued for defamation – and won. Needless to say, it is no small feat to win a defamation lawsuit in California, where anyone can Yelp their mouths off with impunity, under the guise of "opinion." Upon appeal, however, it was determined that TU was a limited public figure and Donald Trump would have had to prove malice in order to prevail. Legally speaking, malice means "actual malice," which is defined as either (publishing the information) knowing it is false, or [sic] with reckless disregard for truth. As everything in Makaeff's complaint was based on her experience and opinion, Donald Trump could not possibly prove she did not have this opinion or knew that the information about him was false – he would have had to prove the value of the courses met with Makaeff's satisfaction. Thus, the lower court ruling was negated and TU ordered (by the infamous La Raza judge Curiel) to pay Makaeff's legal fees of approx. $800,000.

In the meantime, in reaction to the publicity created by Makaeff, a class action lawsuit was filed under CAFA (Class Action Fairness Act) alleging fraud, false advertising, abuse of elders (as some of the course participants were over 60, even 65 years old), RICO violations and other claims in excess of $5mil. Makaeff was named as the representative plaintiff for the class, but dropped out as soon as she had received her defamation payout. Donald Trump moved to dismiss the suit but judge Curiel denied the motion.

Other plaintiffs arose like mushrooms after rain as soon as the attorneys published the action and set up a site where they could sign up as litigants against TU. One of the attorneys' main arguments was that TU was operated with intent to defraud and that all the positive reviews Donald Trump produced (to counter the accusations against him and this venture) had been provided under pressure. Thus, as of now, these class action attorneys claim, every student of TU has the right for triple statutory damages (3x$35,000) plus punitive and other damages.

First year law students learn the law of contracts, which contains the definition of "promise," "consideration," and that "puffing" does not constitute a valid "promise." We all know this from T.V. commercials: "Buy My Pillow, the best pillow in the world. You will sleep like a little baby..." If I do not, can I sue? Hardly. However, if the seller says that "his pillow" contains goose feathers and it does not, I will have a cause of action. Here is another example: compare "My car is a chick magnet. You're sure to meet your future wife in it," with: "My car can do 60mph in 3 seconds. Its mileage is 50 miles per gallon." In order for a promise to create legal liability, it must be based in fact, possible to disprove, and the buyer must have relied on it to its detriment (causing damages).

In order to prevail in this action, Donald Trump will have to show is that his advertising was simple "puffery" (similar to the "pillow talk" of the famous T.V. "pillow guy") and that the students could not have expected to become "real estate magnates" (note the vagueness of such a "promise") – in particular at the age of 65 when they had never done any real business before.

The lawsuit quotes from the Trump University website, where Donald Trump states:

> "Trump University grew out of my desire to impart my business knowledge, accumulated over the

years, and my realization that there is a huge demand for practical, convenient education that teaches success. I want the people who go to Trump University to succeed, and I plan to do my part to help them. I'm not just putting my name on this venture; I plan to be an active presence in the curricula. The website, www.trumpuniversity.com, will include such features as "Ask Mr. Trump," in which I answer your questions; the blog you're reading now; video clips of me; and more. My words, ideas, and image will also be woven into the courses we create. The reason I'm playing such an active role in Trump University is that I truly believe in the power of education . . . . [T]he people who go to Trump University want to be successful, and I'm on their side."

Is this puffery or false advertising? The court will decide. However, as a former professor with passion for teaching, I feel for Donald Trump. Back in Europe, I co-founded the first MENSA Grammar School in Central Europe, where I also taught for three years. Teaching is something I love doing. Every teacher is blessed many times: by imparting her knowledge with self-pride and a sense of achievement, blessed by seeing the students learn and grow, blessed by their power of knowledge, their newly achieved self-reliance, independence, and – often – gratitude. Why, when I was leaving to become a university professor, I even had students line up in front of my office asking me not to leave! I was also blessed every time I met with the parents who trusted me and relied on my knowledge and skills in helping their child. A few years ago, I toyed with the idea of setting up a similar school here in California, but what hurdles would I have to clear in order to obtain accreditation – if even Donald Trump failed in this regard...?!

It took Donald Trump 40 years, perhaps three generations, to develop and establish his name. It is worth a lot of money and he has the right to use it for advertising.

He also possesses the experience you would not obtain anywhere else, so you may opt for your local community college for $200/course or for Trump University for $20,000. At the end of the day, you must learn and study and try and fail – on your own, by yourself. It seems to me that today's mentality is that somehow someone will come to the student and pour it into their thick skull and they will become an instant genius commensurate to how much they have paid. By the way, has anyone heard about Clinton's "Laurate University" which charges $60,000?

Education is business. All Ivy League universities are probably $500,000 plus expenses per degree. Of course, they will keep tabs on competition and pull strings with the government whenever grants and subsidies, accreditations and degrees are concerned. You should see the departmental upheaval when a grant is offered of a million or two for a particular project for a particular university: the faculty gathers and everyone is told what to say to the grant committee in order to obtain the money. The head of the department is "pulling strings" with colleagues who know the grant committee members and then, when everything is brought to a successful conclusion, the money is used for bonuses for the staff (corresponding to the strict departmental hierarchy), a new printer-copier, secretary's desk, even vacations...

It seems to me that the difference between e.g. Harvard and Trump University was that TU was not accredited and did not have a campus – not in the promises made or professors hired. Perhaps he should have written Art of the Deal II instead...

Trump's Foreign Policy Speech

Last week, Donald Trump had his first "presidential" appearance when he gave his "foreign policy speech." He has been attacked for being ambivalent, yet conforming to the Cold War standard of U.S. world hegemony. The criticism of his speech both in the United States as well as abroad has been prompt and sweeping.

"I can only hope that the election campaign in the USA does not lack the perception of reality," Frank-Walter Steinmeier said. "The world's security architecture has changed," Germany's Secretary of State continued. "It is no longer based on two pillars alone. It cannot be conducted unilaterally. No American president can get round this change in the international security architecture... 'America first' is actually no answer to that."

Interestingly, Germany itself has taken the "right turn" as left-wing demonstrators are being suppressed and the conservative AfD is gaining momentum. "Germany First" is in the hearts of the German people, but what can they do – the burden of history weighs heavy on their shoulders, and Mrs. Merkel knows it.

Carl Bildt, a former Swedish prime minister and foreign minister who served as UN envoy to the Balkans in the aftermath of the Yugoslav wars of the 1990s, said he heard that Trump was "abandoning both democratic allies and democratic values."

However, Sweden itself is now paying the price, realizing that "democratic" does not mean "socialist" and that "socialist democracy" is not democracy but chaos at best – socialism at worst. Sweden is offering $1,500 to any and every Muslim immigrant who is willing to voluntarily leave the country. A new series of violent armed Muslim riots have occurred last week in Sweden. Rapes continue. Muslims poison Swedish dogs with "laced sausages," vandalize Christmas trees (they call it "celebrating Christmas") and only two days ago, when Christians entered a Muslim refugee area with charitable and peaceful purposes, they were tied up, dressed in white robes, paraded in public, ordered to kneel down and their heads were chopped off with a machete! You can find pictures of this and other atrocities on the internet. This is happening in Sweden NOW!

Yet, they are criticizing Trump, who wants to keep us safe! Newspapers and internet media are teeming with headlines such as (the) "First Isolationist Candidate" who is "withdrawing support from our friends..." Let us look into what Trump really said and how much truth there is in this mass media phobia and pro-socialist pandering.

Trump made several good points in his speech. First, he criticized Obama's conciliatory gestures and empty rhetoric, especially with respect to his lack of support for the uprising against Mubarak in Egypt in 2011 and his vacuous threat of a "red line" against Assad. He also attacked the "nuclear deal" with Iran, a major thorn in the eye to Israel as well as Turkey and Saudi Arabia.

Second, Trump promised "a disciplined, deliberate and consistent foreign policy," as opposed to the "reckless, rudderless and aimless" policies of Obama and former Secretary of State Hillary Clinton. One of the key points, which somehow escaped (perhaps deliberately?) the attention of the German and Swedish ministers, was Trump's reassertion of our nuclear defense system over Europe, which was dismantled by Obama in 2009, even as Iran had already had the capacity to reach Warsaw and Prague and Budapest with their nuclear-loaded intercontinental missiles. Trump's speech proposed that the systems over Poland and the Czech Republic (once much acclaimed and praised by the locals – to which I am a personal witness) be reinstalled and expanded.

Next, Donald Trump proposed that NATO allies should spend at least 2 percent of their respective GDPs on defense. Tacitly, Obama has taken up this suggestion and made it an official point of his pro-NATO policies. This "rhetoric" raised alarm among all countries that still rely on the United States for defense – including South Korea and Japan. What happened? They are reluctant to contribute to the defense of their own countries?!

Former South Korean Vice Foreign Minister Kim Sung-han, who now teaches at the Korea University in Seoul, said Trump would be "the first isolationist to be U.S. presidential candidate, while in the post-war era all the U.S. presidents have been to varying degrees internationalists."

Obviously, all these politicians have their countries' interests in mind. Donald Trump has ours. As to the "post-war era," from Marshall Plan to Yugoslavia to Iran, we have always attempted to help our friends, no matter what the price! However, let us examine the veracity of these "various degrees of internationalism" with respect to our entire history.

It was George Washington who had cautioned us against "entangling alliances," a phrase hallowed by Thomas Jefferson in his Inaugural address. Monroe Doctrine, which told Europe "hands off, America is ours," is a flip coin of the same mint. When Tsar Alexander II put down the Polish uprising in 1863, French Emperor Napoleon III asked the United States to "join in a protest to the Tsar." Secretary of State William H. Seward responded that our foreign policy was that of "non-intervention...forbearing at all times, and in every way, from foreign alliances, intervention, and interference."

Panama, Nicaragua and the Middle East were not included in the Monroe Doctrine, but Roosevelt in his famous Corollary of 1904 made it clear to Europe that the U.S. "Big Stick Policy" would enforce European claims outside Europe, perhaps everywhere but the Middle East. This Mahan-Machiavelli declaration was gnawing on Woodrow Wilson's progressivist conscience, but even he had been famously carried on into his second term on the echoes of the motto "He kept US out of war!" Then the Germans sank Lusitania...

Nonetheless, a real turn from our fundamental native (and, by the same token, perhaps "nativist") policy of isolationism did not come until Pearl Harbor. Lusitania, Pearl Harbor, Bay of Pigs, 9/11... no-one will be isolationist when attacked on their native soil. As Christians, we have one more cheek, but we are no cowards and we will not be intimidated. I do not think anyone needs to fear American "isolationism."

What is more, the world is more of a closer, tumultuous place today than ever in the past. It is itself unpredictable, and thus predicting a policy which will react to unpredictability cannot itself be called predictable. There are only guidelines; and, as a guideline, national security is a good policy. An insecure nation can never prosper.

The only solution to the instability of all nations lies in returning to their roots and focusing on their domestic growth and well-being. This mean global capitalism, founded on personal improvement and private property – the very opposite of global socialization and "communization" of nations. Nations refuse to be "communized." We are all different.

When Xenia Wickett, head of the "U.S. and Americas Programme" at Britain's Chatham House "think tank" said that Trump's policies would "make America's allies less secure rather than more," this statement reflects her socialist bias – reliance on some magical wand the United States will wave to make Britain safe.

British Prime Minister David Cameron called Trump "divisive, stupid and wrong," which reminds me of Obamaesque "police acted stupidly." Police acted as they had to under the circumstances. So will we; and, as Machiavelli would say, may those unwilling to be our friends – fear US!

Merry Christmas

We live in a culture of plenty. Few, if any, people really starve and live on the street. If they do, it is often by choice or weakness, result of drug addiction, disintegrated family and poor education. Even the poor in our country have one or two cars, a family house, and enough to eat all year round.

We live in a culture of diminishing expectations, where the average is just enough, everyone gets a trophy, and no-one demands the best, lest they should be accused of discrimination or some "phobia." Nonetheless, most of us still keep trying our best without being forced.

We also live in a culture craving and desperate for myths and rituals, as we have seen in the recent demand for a fantastic sequel to Star Wars. Superstition often substitutes religion, because we all must believe in something. Star Wars series fill a void in atheists and agnostics...

No wonder there are so few protests and so little concern in the mainstream media when a principal bans Santa and Merry Christmas in public schools turns into Happy Holidays, and the Bethlehem scene in a shopping mall is replaced with an irregular iceberg symbolizing climate change. Ideology of the left, their political correctness and politics are forced upon us everywhere we go.

Instead of Uncle Scrooge, our "Happy Holidays" tales are supposed to be about "Uncle Plenty" in the form and shape of an aged man with glasses who enjoins us to "Spread the Wealth!" and "Attack Wall Street!" Instead of forgiving Holy Mary we are supposed to look up to the strained, poor actress with a halo around her head painted by the DNC: "Worship me because I am a woman!" Meanwhile, blame goes around – and comes around.

It is no wonder that we are becoming listless, numb, tired of politics to the point of surrender. May this "Holiday" pass in peace... Ah, do you recall the Christmas of our childhood? There were simple presents under the tree, because Christmas was about love and peace and family, and even those presents meant less than the love they represented... There was a resplendent yet simple dinner with the whole family, Christmas carols on the radio, room filled with gentle air of family cohesion and national unity. Evil was on the outside only – and we were always able to put the past behind us and unite against it!

Merry Christmas! Not "happy" but "merry," and it is more than a "holiday." Christmas does not mean a break from work or more time to waste vacationing. If we travel, we travel for love, to love. That is what Christmas is about: love, peace, happiness and plenty.

At this time of the year, in all the nations around the world, families gather and celebrate the birth of Jesus Christ: Christmas means the Christ's Mass. Epiphany means the revelation of the Son of God in a human being, Jesus Christ. Have you had an epiphany? One is coming...

To celebrate means to remember where we come from, where we are and how fortunate we have been to have come so far. We must celebrate our health and wealth and even the demands that the world poses upon us, because the meaning of life is in what we do for others.

We do not need to create new rituals and crave for new world orders, different religions or political systems – all we need to do is to scratch our puppy, turn off the TV sometimes, sit down in a quiet room and muse. Socrates could muse for days: standing still in cold weather without food or water. Jesus was even stronger. Our strength lies in our love, our willpower, and our unity.

Some of us may not know how to pray, but there is nothing to a prayer. A prayer can be completely "secular" – because it is the expression of the happiness of the soul, unity with Nature, gratitude for where we are – here and now; and, as Winston Churchill said, that is all we need to succeed in life. Merry Christmas!

Sen. Cruz Warns:
Orwellian Censorship of Obama's Administration Poses Grave Risk to Our National Security

You may have watched Senator Cruz two days ago on CSPAN 2, during the concluding remarks in the hearing on radical Islam and terrorism in the Senate Judiciary Subcommittee on Oversight and Federal Courts. He made only three observations, but were they worth the while!

First, Senator Cruz said: "Any religion which kills members of another religion is hostile to our civilization!" This was a reaction to the Democrat committee members' comparing ISIS to KKK. Senator Cruz cited Dr. Martin Luther King's "Letter from Birmingham Jail," which begins "My Dear Fellow Clergymen," speaking to all people regardless of faith or denomination. One might speak of a "Church of Humanity..." The underlying motif Senator Cruz wanted to emphasize was twofold: if members of one faith speak only to that faith, spiting all other faiths, that in itself is bigotry; and, as Dr. King expressed his "disappointment with the Church" in his 1963 Letter, Senator Cruz was likewise expressing his disappointment with his Democrat colleagues.

Senator Cruz's disappointment was amplified by the fiasco of a soliloquy by President Obama during the so-called "Three Amigos" meeting in Canada: Nieto-Trudeau-Obama – the Socialist Trojka of the West concluded with Obama's thinly veiled criticism of Donald J. Trump: "...some people who have never created jobs... who do not think of people, do not care for people... call themselves populists." Many questions arise, of course, from Obama's "shovel-ready" jobs to the deceit perpetrated upon our Nation in Obamacare subterfuge, Benghazi negligence etc. How can someone assume that someone else does not care – unless, of course, they announce it to the world openly, e.g. "What difference does it make if four young men are murdered because of my negligence and I lie to their families...?"

Senator Cruz's eyes filled with sadness, weight of responsibility, yet powerlessness over the status quo, as he proceeded to the second point in his speech, expressing extreme "disappointment" at the "purge" conducted by the Administration in all reports regarding Islamic Terrorism. Obama's administration deleted the word "Jihad" over and again in every single military and law enforcement report. What troubled Senator Cruz above all else, he stated, was that the "Orwellian censorship of law enforcement materials" remained "of no concern" to his colleagues. "The Senate has a long history of holding the Executive accountable, and should express a real concern about censorship of law enforcement materials," Senator Cruz emphatically concluded.

1984 flashes in my mind – does anyone read Orwell anymore? "Freedom is slavery. Ignorance is strength." Does this not sound like AG Lynch when she said that the only way to fight terrorists is to love them? How Christian of her... (pardon my sarcasm). Yet Obama forces upon US on average 2,000 Syrian Muslims a month without any vetting! 80% of them want Sharia Law. 20% of them are statistically likely to be Islamic Fascists (Jihadist adherents of ISIS). At the same time, we are facing a possibility of Clinton-Warren ticket! Only the ignorant or the indoctrinated could vote for this Snowball-Napoleon déjà vu (viz. Animal Farm) – two pigs greedy for power, squeaking: "Some animals are more equal than others!"

Finally, Senator Cruz pointed out that, to his great surprise, distress and dismay, none of his Democrat colleagues expressed any concern about how the Administration repeatedly, from Little Rock to Chattanooga to San Bernardino to Boston to Orlando, ignored and passed over terrorist attacks, which were entirely preventable - were it not for government purges and political correctness, which ties the hands of our law enforcement as well as the military. Instead of calling the Evil by its name – "radical Islamic terrorism" – Obama's administration has been "playing with semantics," said Senator Cruz. "It is not a question of semantics," he continued firmly, "but of acknowledgement of threat."

It is astounding to me that even such a capacity on Islam as Dr. Jasser Zuhdi, founder of the Islamic Center for Pluralism, was treated by the Democrats on the Committee in a tone of dismissive disparagement when he stated that there is no difference between being "inspired" by ISIS and being a "member" or "follower" of ISIS. In particular, his point was that calling Evil what it is - "radical Islamic terrorism" - would actually help the "good Muslims" unite and "clear the house of Islam" of the filth of Islamic fascism.

My ears perked up when Senator Cruz mentioned how Obama's administration is "purging" official reports and documents, because the verb "to purge" and the noun "a purge" looms large in the mind of anyone acquainted with socialism/communism. Purge? The socialist-communist-democrat party must be "purged" of disbelievers! Anyone doubtful of their ideology, anyone suggesting more plurality (like Dr. Zuhdi) or – God forbid! – constitutionalism – must be purged!

So far they are purging only our language, but beware, for purges do not end with language!

Who Is the New Mayor of London?

Sadiq Aman Khan is 46 years old. He was born in London, fifth of eight children to a Sunni Muslim family of Pakistani immigrants. As he publicly declared, his family continues to "send money to relatives in Pakistan... because we're blessed living in this country." However, one might also ask: how does he pay back to the country which bestowed such blessings upon him?

As soon as Mr. Khan obtained his law degree, he focused on employment and discrimination law, taking up cases of "oppressed Muslims," such as Ahmed v. University of Oxford (2002). In this case, three students took an exam in Arabic: one was white and two were non-white. The white student, Ms. Clark, passed, but the non-white student, Mr. Ahmed failed. Dr. Zimmermann, their examiner, was sued for discrimination against the non-white student under the Race Relations Act of 1976. Mr. Khan took up Mr. Ahmed's defense. The Crown Court ruled against Mr. Ahmed, who said he was "flabbergasted and shocked," and appealed the decision based on "bias" and "unfairness" – to spite Oxford University, which issued a statement to the effect that the "case should never have been brought" and that it is one of the "most diverse and multicultural institutions in England" (a statement with which anyone who has ever visited Oxford would no doubt whole-heartedly agree). Mr. Kahn appealed and fought on, asserting this Muslim student's rights for another two years. I wonder if Mr. Ahmed, a graduate enrollee in an MA program in Medieval Arabic could not have perhaps prepared better and retake the exam...?

In another case, Dr. Jadhav v. Secretary of State for Health, Mr. Khan sued the Department of Health based on racial discrimination against Indian doctors. In this case, Dr. Jadhav, a physician born in India who had obtained his degree in Bombay, was refused training in England on the grounds that his visa would run out before he could complete the training. After a prolonged trial, Department of Health considered appeal more costly than settlement, and gave Mr. Khan and Dr. Jadhav 635,000 GBP to make the case go away.

Mr. Khan has also always enjoyed suing the police for racial discrimination. Most notably, in CI Logan v. Met police, the Chief Inspector, chairman of the Metropolitan Black Police Association (MBPA) was accused of filing a false claim for a hotel bill. Mr. Khan alleged that the case against Logan was made up against him because of his support of an Iranian-born superintendent Ali Dizaei who was charged with dishonesty at the Old Bailey. Mr. Dizaei won the case against him and Inspector Logan was cleared of all impropriety. Consequently, Mr. Khan gained more notoriety in the media and could move on to even more controversial cases, such as suing the police under the Human Rights Act during the tumultuous communist Mayday demonstration in 2001, suing the Met Police for false imprisonment (DcDowell and Taylor v. Met Police) or defending Mr. Farrakhan against the Home Secretary.

Farrakhan v. Home Secretary can be cited here as a case in point for Mr. Khan's staunch defense of radical Muslims. Louis Farrakhan, was born as Louis Wolcott. He was first known as Louis X (professing "X" for his allegedly "slave heritage"). He learned Koran by heart and changed his name to Muhammad after his conversion and acceptance to the Nation of Islam (NOI), one of the largest racist Muslim groups in the United States. He also took up the moniker Farrakhan as a "holy name" (which in Arabic means "the Criterion" or "Al Furquan" and references Quran itself). Farrakhan alias Furquan is currently the leader of the Nation of Islam, minister of major mosques in Boston and Harlem, and even the Southern Poverty Law Center describes him as "anti-Semitic and proponent of anti-white theology." He has been widely known for being homophobic and preaching hatred of white people. He is also fond of scientology and advocate of Hubbard's "auditing" techniques for all his disciples.

Mr. Khan defended the racist Muslim Jihadist Muhammad X Farrakhan Al Furquan when the British Home Department denied him entry to the United Kingdom, on the grounds that his presence would exacerbate tensions between the Jewish and Muslim communities. How this dispute ended is apparent from the fact that Mr. Khan has been elected as the Mayor of the City of London.

There are numerous other cases, many of which involve fake "students," illegal immigrants and radical Muslims sentenced for deportation by the Department of State. Mr. Khan defended them all, mostly with great success and to his current renown and acclaim.

As attorneys, we sometimes have to take cases of clients whose claims are not clear-cut, because facts are often not black-and-white. However, there is something wrong with lawyers who see only black and for whom Good and Evil are mere political causes. I wonder if the people of London really know whom they entrusted with their highest office…

There Can Be No Capitalism, No Republic – without Independence

European Union as we know it was not established until 1993 in Maastricht. You may recall that Margaret Thatcher argued strongly against it. People who have opposed the current vote to exit the Union are not familiar with its history. Rather, they have been scared by the big government junkies and politicians who think the world would not turn without their treaties and agreements.

I lived and studied in England from 1990 to 1995. I visited England many times after that, especially when I worked for the European Community in Brussels in 1996-7. I was also employed by the government to teach the history and magnificence of the EU to the employees of the National Bank, Supreme Audit Office and other grand governmental establishments.

I also spent two years traveling and working all over England. From Newcastle to Plymouth, from Exeter to Canterbury, people were proud to be British. They absolutely hated having to abandon their currency, the Pride of their Kingdom, and submit to the government in Brussels. They were proud of their "splendid insulation," their independence from "the Continent." They would say: "That's the way we do it, not like on the Continent," placing a disparaging accent on the last word...

Subsequently, I worked in Brussels at the very core of the European Union, Directorate Generale 1. To my surprise and bewilderment, I had a very similar experience with Belgian people, who absolutely hate and detest the EU government, which, they say, sucks them dry and leaves them out – EU officials' starting salary is 3 times that of an average Belgian citizen. They travel by cabs and shop in special stores around the EU district. Belgian people in that district are better off – from *boulangeries* to pharmacies to clothes and shoe stores... "They look down on us," my Belgian friend told me. "People like you," she continued, "they come and go, well dressed, caring nothing for what we want." How "common Americans" feel about Washington D.C. today, it seems to me, is very similar...

From the Coal and Steel Community in 1952, EU has developed not just into a single market area with free movement of goods, but also into the Schengen passport-free area without borders. There is no doubt in my mind that this development (especially the 2009 Lisbon Treaty, which created a "legal personality" and a host of unelected, permanent officials, growing the government in Brussels ever larger) contributed significantly to the current development. Had there been no Schengen, there would have been no Muslim Invasion.

Just like Obama in 2009, European Union in 2012 received the Nobel Peace Prize for "having contributed to the advancement of peace and reconciliation, democracy and human rights in Europe." How absurd is this? First, they give it to a novice politician with no record of achievement but a trail of apologies which caused the rise of Terrorism and Islamic Fascism in the world; then to a body politic (for lack of a better term) for something accomplished by FDR, Truman and Reagan (end of World War II and Cold War). Will the gathering of senile professors in Stockholm be taken by surprise when Sweden referendum falls the way the British did?

There is no capitalism without independence. There is no republic in a borderless world of universal socialism. The Muslim Invasion of Europe was the last straw. I am only surprised that it has taken so long...

Doping in Sport

Russian athletes' doping scandal has been overshadowed by the recent terrorist attacks in Paris. They are not, however, unconnected. All Russian athletes are now facing Olympic suspension. This means suspending Russia. As a former Olympic athlete who represented an Eastern Bloc country in the days of Cold War boycotts, I remember how I felt when the 1984 Olympic Games in Los Angeles were "boycotted" by Warsaw Pact countries and how we felt about the games in Soul. Our focus stayed on "local" competitions, Nationals, Europe, perhaps the World, if organized in a country which the Party did not view as a severe "flight risk." It was not uncommon in those days that a bus of athletes going to compete in France or West Germany would return half empty, with four Secret Police Agents forced to explain what had happened…

Ancient Olympic Games had been held every four years at the sanctuary of Zeus in Olympia, Greece. They date as far back as 776 BC and the events (equestrian, athletic, wrestling, boxing and throws) celebrated and substituted for military ventures and achievements. Very likely, they commemorated and celebrated the conquest of Troy and the adventures described in Homer's Iliad. During the games, all hostilities and wars were suspended and postponed – the idea passed down to us as the "Olympic Peace."

Interestingly, Modern Olympic Games began as a celebration of Greek victory of independence from the Ottoman Empire in 1821. The conflict between the East and West is as old as civilization itself. Ever since Baron Pierre de Coubertin founded the International Olympic Committee (IOC) in 1894 – in Paris – the ideas of equality and fairness have stood out indelibly in every athlete's mind. The Olympic Creed states that: "The most important thing" is "not to win but to take part, just as the most important thing in life is not the triumph but the struggle." This places the "struggle" on parallel to the metaphysical "journey" through life – the victory should not matter: "The essential thing is not to have conquered but to have fought well," said Baron de Coubertin.

However, you cannot fight well if you are not fighting to win. What is more, it is not just athletes who are fighting but the nations themselves. The Olympic Movement is a massive, expensive venture today with the opening ceremonies running to $100mil and companies investing (and making) billions on the Games. It is no wonder that the idea of "peace" has been substituted by the notion of the "journey" – because the content is hardly peaceful. It is a struggle at every step, personal, team-wise, national endeavor – and it never ends. The journey is thorny and the eyes are on the prize, not on the thorns. "Take what you have to, do what you must!" sounds more like a modern Olympic motto that National Teams' coaches would use. They certainly did in my days...

Many of us are familiar with anabolic steroids, because they are the most frequent and also the most obvious of doping substances. Depending on the sport, however, there are many other agents, most notably stimulants, beta-blockers, and relaxing agents, such as marihuana and many medications considered therapeutic are on the prohibited WADA list. When you are an athlete competing in one of the many IOC recognized sports, you have to be on the lookout even when you are buying over-the-counter supplements and substances generally available to everybody (for instance, DHEA on your local Ralph's shelves, is a substance whose positive blood/urine finding may result in the athlete's being banned for life).

When I was on the Olympic Team, there were no protein, supplements and little was known about nutrition. We had vitamins and mineral drinks during workouts. While nutritional science and supplementation has advanced significantly, the recent news from Russia clearly shows that little has changed in terms of training "techniques" and structure: you must obey or you will be "terminated!" Only the coach knows what is good for you. Of course, in my "Olympic days" it was exacerbated by the fact that we lived in communism. There was no way you could say "no" to the comrade coach – they have the power over you and your family!

Communism is gone from the map, but you cannot erase it from the hearts and minds of the people. Putin will always have a KGB agent's heart and an Olympic coach will always feel that he is the Comrade-in-Chief, the pastor to his pride. He is – if only because he is one of the "insiders," that is to say those who have "ties" and can pull "strings" for you. The recent 350-page Pound/McLaren WADA Report reveals that there has been a "vast doping program," athletes were injected by the "team" doctor (Sergei Portugalov) and the cover-up originated in the lab and athletes who wanted "out" were extorted (the marathon runner Shobukhova paid $520,000 to Russian officials for "clearance").

From my own experience, I can tell you that there is no way that a coach of the Olympic Team would not know when WADA is testing and what is the likelihood of individual random tests at particular time of the year. Further, national WADA affiliates will usually contact the head coach or the lab first. It does not take that much (in terms of bribes or acquaintance) to establish "ties" to the lab and the national testing body. A whole "underground trade" develops, in which athletes are just pawns in the game, paying for their ignorance or negligence. At the end of the day, under the barrage of questions, the team doctor may tell you what you have just taken or been injected with, but, by then, it is usually too late.

Most athletes do not take performance enhancing substances willfully or even knowingly. There are those who are forced to turn a blind eye to what they take – or be ostracized and expelled – and there are those who make an honest mistake. You cannot judge unless you know the circumstances. Banning them all by a strike of the WADA pen, as has just happened is grossly unfair. Imagine you have been working out every day 4-6 hours for ten, fifteen years of your life and you have one, maybe two chances at the Olympics. You took what they gave you because you trusted the coach. Indeed, he has been the only person with genuine authority and interest in your advancement. Parents are far away – it is your team members and your coach who are your family now…

I recall that on average we swam 50-60 kilometers a week. Add several hours in the gym, plus running, basketball, football – twice a week. When you can think of something else, some goal in the future, some way of getting out, surviving "this" – you can "leave your body" and stop feeling the pain. It is not the best way to the Olympic podium, but it is often the only way to survive. There were people who did not – about one half "dropped out" during the first year, another one third in the second. Some could not handle the educational requirements and had to repeat the year (provided that you were a particularly successful athlete, of course, your study records could be overlooked – but such was rare). Our class was a mixture of older and younger athletes, 14-18 at any given time, from three different sports: track-and-field, gymnastics, and swimming.

It was very much like an army division – we all knew one another well, naked to the bone mentally as well as physically. When we traveled for competitions and meets we were constantly under supervision and stuck together – against every outsider. I imagine we looked weird to the people "on the outside" – if only because they looked "weird" to us. What is more, we were not permitted to go outside the permitted perimeter of the sleeping and workout facilities or speak with anyone, especially not about our training techniques or testing. Yes, we had our own team of doctors who would come to pierce our fingers for blood sampling (red and white blood count during exertion), urine tests, CO_2 and oxygen consumption testing… you name it. The coach would know exactly what event our body was best suited for.

Very few of us knew what was in the pills we were given as "vitamins" during workouts, but they seemed to help. The bucketful of "ion drink" for the team was also a godsend, because workouts lasted for 3 hours in the morning and 3 hours in the evening. Once, I refused to take the pills. Everybody took them. I left mine on the bulkhead.

Comrade Coach, the National Team Head Coach (whose favorite yell – till my ears popped – was "You'll be here till I see you sweating blood!!!") frowned and shouted at me that the State paid for these and I should realize how "privileged" I was, etc. etc. I learned to pull the One-Flew-over-the-Cuckoo's-Nest stunt. Unlike others, I did not trust the 350-pound sadist who "broke" my knees (as he proudly stated – to teach me the proper breaststroke kick position) by forcing me to lie down prone on the floor bending my legs as he leaned on them and pushed on the inside of my ankles with all his weight…

The journey was hard and long. I took no shortcuts. Either you can do it – or not. There is no pill in the world will make you a world champion!

Listening to the news from Russia, I am not surprised. The demand and pressure must be even higher now: the "prestige" and renown are even greater and even more money is involved. Further, with globalization of the news and electronic mass media and the ability to instantly communicate not only the results but also techniques, methods, supplementation etc. athletes feel more empowered, more knowledgeable, perhaps, in some cases, manipulating the system. However, is such knowledge not a blindfold over what really matters?

Nutrition is better and legal supplementation is fabulous! We had had no protein powders, pre- and after-workout drinks filled with "aminos," creatine, glutamine, carnitine… All we had was a thick slice of bread with lard for breakfast, fat soaked burgers for lunch and pancakes loaded with sugar for supper. Had they given us a Subway sandwich with all that good meat and veggies and a quart of milk a day – why, I may have won the Olympics!

After I left the Team, I encountered people (I cannot call them "athletes") who used two or three oral steroids and two or three injectable ones. Other banned substances most commonly abused are stimulants and diuretics. Especially stimulants are becoming more problematic and WADA is considering banning coffee and caffeine drinks (Coke). Quite frankly, it amazes me when I stand in line in Subway how casually people guzzle down "energy drinks" as they nervously kick into the wall and yell on the phone... I split such a drink in two and use it as a pre-workout stimulant, not more than twice a week because the body gets used to everything and the effect decreases.

The list of banned substances is annually renewed and it is the athlete's (not the coach's responsibility to review it). The penalties are so severe and the stigma attached to any transgression so great that I cannot imagine any Olympic athlete would willfully take a banned substance. I was shocked when I saw Michael Phelps smoking marihuana. Not only is marihuana prohibited, but smoking anything is terrible for a swimmer who must rely on maximum lung capacity. It pains me even more because Michael was someone who I admired, from "my" sport.

Today, an Olympic athlete should be the ambassador of a healthy lifestyle, fighting against drug use and addiction which has ruined too many of our youth. After all, we athletes know about addiction perhaps more than anybody: is sport itself not an addiction above all others? I am addicted to the struggle, the everyday victory over myself. I want to taste the bitter with the sweet. If you cannot stand pain and all you think of is shortcuts, there is no room for you in sport. That is also why sport is the greatest character builder – and drugs the greatest character destroyer. I would not hesitate to invite to my home an Olympic athlete from any sport, no matter how briefly I knew them. Real athletes do not steal, rob or murder – or take drugs.

Pierre de Coubertin's Olympic Ideal is about the journey and how we athletes pave the way for the others to follow and reach: faster, higher, stronger! At some point in the athletic career, one will cease to represent just oneself. Young people and public at large (or simply our immediate friends and fans, however small the group may be) will look up to us as heroes, someone who fought and conquered – and it is our obligation to show them that it is not about the point of conquest but about the journey which took us there. We must have fought fair and square all the way, because otherwise both the journey and its goal are meaningless. It is the role of every athlete to preserve the dignity of their sport and the Olympic Ideal, which says that peace only comes to those who have fought well – fought in a square field with a like foe; fought to the best of their ability – no matter what the outcome of the fight may be.

Peyton Manning v. Al Jazeera

Al Jazeera's reporter Deborah Davies reaffirmed the allegation that growth hormone was being sent to Peyton Manning's wife in Florida. Apparently, the recanting "source" – aptly called "Sly" – was credible after all... Middle Eastern journalistic "culture" has reached our continent!

"The only allegation in the program from Charlie Sly is that growth hormone was sent repeatedly from Guyer (Institute) to Ashley Manning in Florida," Davies said. "We're not making the allegation against Peyton Manning." Of course, denying what you are saying while actually saying it is a typical example of Doublespeak, something we know only too well from socialist populists.

At law, implying something by saying something else is called "slander by innuendo." Although politicians seem to be exempt from any and all forms of malpractice today, every journalist must verify credibility of their sources. We have had the occasion to witness the undesirable ripple effect of wrongful allegations in some rape college cases lately. "Journalistic malpractice" is simple negligence, no different from having a drunk or unskilled plumber cause a flood in your house.

Further, one should not be afraid to reveal to his or her physician the use of any substances which may affect proposed treatment, including drugs. We have seen what personal uncertainty and insecurity any leak of such personal information may cause when the news came about Obamacare website having been hacked and personal data stolen. Unfortunately, physician-patient privilege has not yet been included in the Federal Rules of Evidence. Nonetheless, every state has some form of physician-patient privilege in force.

As a professional athlete, I have often been amazed what prejudice and misunderstanding circulates in public with regard to "prohibited substances." WADA is actually considering prohibiting coffee as we speak. As the repercussions would be from the multi-million dollar industry

(CocaCola, boost and sports drinks, etc.), such a ban is unlikely.

WADA Prohibited List is 10 pages long and extensive enough, updated each year, and it is every athlete's personal responsibility to review it and know it. Nonetheless, many of the substances and methods of doping prohibited by WADA are commonly used in everyday medical care. Steroids are routinely administered after traumatic injuries, to cancer patients, patients with pituitary malfunctions, postmenopausal women... Hardly a day passes without a "Low-T Therapy" commercial on T.V.! I have recently, been taken aback by a 60+year-old colleague of mine who confided in me that he felt "like born again!" He was "undergoing an 'HG-T treatment' called an 'anti-aging therapy'," he whispered into my ear. "You should try it! My wife and I can't praise it highly enough!"

How would this colleague of mine look at a professional athlete on such "therapy?" One out of a million has the stamina, resolve and will, but also the luck and chance, to participate in the Olympics or be on the NFL as a pro. All athletes suffer dozens of injuries, some more serious than others, and cannot "afford" to just nod to any "shot" by any doctor. As a professional athlete, I had to "keep my nose clean" – literally – I could not even use the prescription nose drops when I had a cold, because the drops contained a precursor of Ephedrine.

Is your lower back sore? Did you pull your shoulder ligaments? You can go to any doctor for a Corticosteroid shot. Not Peyton Manning. Legitimate use of prescription medication may be tolerated by WADA and USADA, but – who would want to run the risk? Subsequent legal expenses and IOC haggling may cost you your career. No wonder Peyton Manning is up in arms against Al Jazeera.

www.ingramcontent.com/pod-product-compliance
Lightning Source LLC
Chambersburg PA
CBHW062135280526
45788CB00001B/179